The Art of Real Estate Appraisal, 2nd Edition

The Complete Guide for Homeowners and Real Estate Professionals

William L. Ventolo, Jr.
Martha R. Williams, J.D.

KAPLAN

PUBLISHING

New York

Published by Kaplan Publishing, a division of Kaplan, Inc.
1 Liberty Plaza, 24th Floor
New York, NY 10006

Printed in the United States of America

June 2008

10 9 8 7 6 5 4 3 2 1

ISBN-13: 978-1-4277-9720-9

Kaplan Publishing books are available at special quantity discounts to use for sales promotions, employee premiums, or educational purposes. Please email our Special Sales Department to order or for more information at kaplanpublishing@kaplan.com, or write to Kaplan Publishing, 1 Liberty Plaza, 24th Floor, New York, NY 10006.

Contents

Preface

Just as financing is essential to almost all real estate transactions, so is the specialized area of appraisal. An appraisal is a supportable opinion of value. A reliable opinion of the value of property is sought for many different reasons. The seller wants to know the value of his or her property to determine an appropriate selling price; the buyer will rely on an accurate appraisal to be sure the property is fairly priced by the seller; and the broker wants to realize the maximum commission on the sale. In addition, financial institutions insist on an appraisal to determine the amount of money they should lend to a loan applicant. Appraisals are also used to determine value for taxation and insurance purposes, as well as for condemnation proceedings.

The Art of Real Estate Appraisal provides a first exposure to the principles and techniques of appraising residential properties. Assuming that the reader has no prior knowledge of appraising, the book is designed to help homeowners, agents, and investors relate appraisal theory and techniques to their practical concerns regarding property value.

Accurate appraising is a highly developed skill, perhaps even an art in some cases, and we have no illusions that we can turn you into a professional appraiser in a handful of pages. We will, however, tell you a little bit about the theory behind appraising, how professional appraisers go about it, and how you can perhaps adapt some of their techniques in making your own rough determination of property value.

Introduction

When property values are rising, there are few complaints or concerns about appraisals. A seller can ask a record high price for the neighborhood—and buyers respond with multiple bids over the asking price. The buyer who "wins" the property is congratulated and starts counting the profit that will result from such a wise investment even before the ink dries on the deed. Did the appraisal indicate a market value less than the sales price? No problem—just remind the appraiser to look at the asking prices of other properties coming on the market (even higher!) and to take that factor into consideration.

When property values start to decline, however, property appraisals receive considerably more interest. Why should the asking prices of other properties be considered? So what if they seem to indicate that the market has taken a downturn? What about all the sales from the peak of the market—last year?

Other factors that add to the consternation of sellers and buyers when the market moves through its usual cyclical changes and values become difficult to predict include interest rates, construction starts, the unemployment rate, and the criteria that lenders use to make loans, among others. Suddenly, appraisers must be licensed or certified and conform to something called the Uniform Standards of Professional Appraisal Practice (USPAP).

The past three decades have seen wild fluctuations in interest rates that would make the current market seem a buyer's paradise, if not for the fact that prices have increased exponentially as interest rates have gone down. The recent drop in property values has been hard on buyers who bought at the market's peak just a few years ago, but in most parts of the country, the lower property values still represent several multiples of what prices were even 10 years ago. Of course, there are always those areas that seem immune to economic forces, with property prices that seem to be at their peak—and then go even higher. Ironically, some of the highest-priced parts of the country tend to be the ones that experience continuing high demand.

But if you did buy your home at the peak of the market and now are dismayed to see other homes like yours selling for prices that are a lot lower than the price you paid, the coup de grace comes when the bill from the tax collector arrives. Somehow, tax collectors know when property values are going up, but seem reluctant to acknowledge that they have gone down. What can you do to convince the tax collector that you paid more than your home's current market value?

How can a homeowner—or prospective homeowner—get a handle on what a home is actually worth? By understanding how market value is determined and how it can be influenced.

The Art of Real Estate Appraisal was written in response to the need for a layman's explanation of the basics of the appraisal process. Readers interested in buying or selling their own home, refinancing their mortgage, or remodeling for value will find this book useful. If you are a homeseller, learning about the appraisal process can help you set a realistic asking price for your property, which will produce a faster sale at a price near that goal. If you are a homebuyer, an understanding of the appraisal process will help you determine a fair offering price for the home you want to buy. A good working knowledge of the basic principles of property valuation should also be helpful when judging the accuracy of your tax assessment or considering a home improvement project.

Because almost every aspect of the real estate industry involves appraising, this book can be a useful learning tool, not only for prospective buyers and sellers, but for brokers, salespeople, mortgage brokers, loan agents, property managers, investors, and others. Knowing the basics of the appraisal process, for example, can help the real estate agent prepare a competitive market analysis (CMA). This is a service performed by the agent for a seller to show the approximate market value range of the seller's property, and by the agent for a buyer to determine the same information. A CMA, as you will learn, is based on the sales comparison approach, one of three methods used by appraisers to form an opinion of real estate value.

This book is not intended to replace the services of a professional appraiser. You won't find all there is to know about appraising by reading this book. But if we can explain how real estate values are determined and what the problems are in arriving at an opinion of a property's fair market value, we will have accomplished our purpose.

Real Estate and Its Appraisal

The most important reason for having real estate appraised is to support a mortgage loan decision by a lender. Buyers and sellers are often convinced that they know the value of what they are getting—or turning over to someone else. It's the lender who needs to be convinced that the property has sufficient value to serve as security (collateral) for the loan the lender is being asked to make. If the owner simply wants to refinance an existing mortgage, the lender will want to make sure that the current market value of the property supports the new loan amount.

There are other reasons to order an **appraisal,** including the following:

- *Distribution of an estate.* This is especially important if one of the heirs plans to purchase the interests of other heirs.

- *Division of property as part of a divorce.* There will need to be a fair division of the equity in the home, particularly if one spouse transfers his or her share to the other spouse.

- *Property tax assessment.* A homeowner who wants to contest the tax assessor's valuation will need an appraisal to back up a claim of a lower value.

- *Reassessment of property value after improvements are made.* Again, the tax assessor's opinion may differ from the homeowner's.

- *Determination of insured value.* A homeowner should always insure property for its full replacement cost, so it is critical to know what that is.

- *Eminent domain proceeding.* If all or part of the property will be taken by a local authority, the property owner will want to be fairly reimbursed.

- *Partition (division) of property held in co-ownership, such as a tenancy in common (TIC).* If the co-owners did not have an appraisal of the separate ownership interests when they purchased the property, it will be even more important to have one when the property (or part of it) is sold.

- *Determination of salvage value on destruction of property.* Tornadoes, earthquakes, hurricanes, floods, landslides, and vandalism can all have economic repercussions for the homeowner.

- *Asset valuation in a transfer of corporate assets.* Business assets can be a critical part of the sale or transfer of a corporation.

While there are a multitude of reasons to have property appraised, the majority of appraisals are performed to assure a lender of the underlying value of the property used as security for a loan. This means that a real estate appraisal is performed most often to find the market value of the property—that is, what a buyer is likely to pay for it—and that's the type of appraisal we focus on in this book.

WHAT IS A REAL ESTATE APPRAISAL?

A lot of people can give you an opinion of what your house is worth, but a formal appraisal is a *supportable* opinion of property value. An appraisal will include a description of the property being appraised and the **appraiser**'s opinion of the property's condition, its utility for a stated purpose, and its probable monetary value on the open market. Important elements of the appraisal are the qualifications of the appraiser and the validity of the data that forms the basis for the appraiser's determination of value.

The Appraiser

Because the appraisal presents the appraiser's opinion of value, the weight given the appraisal depends on the skill, experience, and good judgment of the appraiser. With an objective, well-researched, and carefully documented appraisal, all parties involved—whether in a sale, mortgage loan, or other transaction—are aided in the decision-making process.

The real estate appraisers who perform most of the appraisals needed for home mortgage loans must be licensed or certified by the state in which the property is located. That wasn't always the case, however. Before 1993, only a few states had any form of appraiser licensing. Some history of the changes in the American economy over the past three decades will help you to understand the importance of today's appraiser licensing regulations, which are a direct result of the savings and loan (S&L) crisis of the 1980s.

Savings and Loan Crisis

According to the Bureau of Labor Statistics, the annual rate of inflation in the United States reached 13.58 percent in 1980. (As a point of comparison, the inflation rate for 2007 was projected in August 2007 at 2.36 percent.) To compete for depositors in a period of high inflation, banks and other lending institutions offered correspondingly high rates on depositor accounts; at one point, it was possible to earn 14 percent interest or more on a one-year certificate of deposit. Even checking accounts became interest-bearing. Of course, to pay those rates to depositors and also cover the costs of doing business, mortgage loans originated in that period carried interest rates that reached historic highs, averaging 17.5 percent in 1982. To put that number in perspective, consider that in October 2007 the average interest rate on a 30-year fixed-rate loan on the median-priced home was 5.94 percent, or about one-third of the rate charged on a comparable loan in 1982.

Savings and loan associations (also referred to as *thrifts*), which at that time were prohibited by federal law from offering products such as interest-bearing checking accounts, lobbied for expansion of their functions. Federal regulators also wanted to bring all commercial banks into the federal banking system. The resulting Depository Institutions Deregulation and Monetary Control Act of 1980 did bring the banks into the federal system, but it also opened the way for more types of interest-bearing deposit accounts across all lending institutions.

The S&Ls thus got what they asked for, but it was a bit like opening Pandora's box. The benefit of offering products such as interest-bearing checking accounts had to be measured against the burden of offering competitive interest rates to depositors at a time of high inflation. To compound the problem, the S&Ls received much of their income from older, long-term, fixed-rate home mortgage loans that paid only a single-digit rate of return, but new depositors expected double-digit interest rates.

The strange nature of doing business as a lending institution in the 1980s caused many institutions to take on risky investments, a certain number of which would have been doomed to failure even in the best economic times. But the 1980s were not the best of times. After the member countries of the Organization of the Petroleum Exporting Countries (OPEC) reduced oil production in the early 1970s and fuel oil and gasoline prices skyrocketed in the United States, the oil industry states experienced a boom time in which investment money poured into new land and offshore development.

By the mid-1980s, however, when international oil production had been expanded and the price of crude oil had dropped, the oil states (Texas, Oklahoma, Colorado, and Louisiana being most prominent) saw the bottom drop out of their commercial expansion and, ultimately, their housing markets. Entire subdivisions in Houston, Texas, which had been a major beneficiary of the oil industry boom, were virtually abandoned. As the oil bust got under way, and before the source of funds dried up, developers were still able to get funds for new developments. It was not unusual for a homeowner to abandon property in one development in order to move into a brand-new home in a development down the road. That state of affairs did not last, however, because the institutions lending the development funds eventually found themselves in trouble.

The collapse of a startling number of S&Ls in the decade that followed revealed that there had been many abusive practices. The sad fact was that faulty and sometimes fraudulent appraisals were at the heart of many ill-conceived financing schemes. In some cases, the appraisals were performed at the request of a lender that was acting in concert with a developer who often had an ownership interest in the lending institution. In one case, an accommodating appraiser in Dallas appraised an office complex for twice its actual value, providing a nice windfall for the developer and the officers of the lending institution. The most egregious examples involved office buildings, but the chicanery was not limited to commercial real estate. In Florida, entire housing tracts were promoted and sold using highly questionable, if not out-and-out falsified, appraisal data.

Certainly, greed was at the core of some of the S&L collapses, but it was not the only factor at work. Many of the problems experienced by the industry stemmed from frantic efforts to compensate for the wild swing in interest rates in an intensely competitive environment by moving to even riskier investments. That trend, unfortunately, did not stop with the collapse of many of the thrifts. We'll touch on current ramifications of that issue in the next chapter.

FIRREA

Congress responded to the savings and loan crisis by passing FIRREA—the Financial Institutions Reform, Recovery, and Enforcement Act of 1989. FIRREA established federal agencies to liquidate the assets of the failed thrifts, which included the sale of many of the residential and commercial properties that had been taken over following loan defaults and foreclosures. The Federal Savings and Loan Insurance Corporation (FSLIC) was abolished and the Federal Deposit Insurance Corporation (FDIC), formerly responsible for insuring only bank deposits, took over FSLIC's insurance responsibilities. The federal bailout of insolvent S&Ls cost the federal government, by one estimate, $153 billion. Taxpayers paid $124 billion of the bailout and the S&L industry paid $29 billion. From 1986 through 1995, the number of federally insured S&Ls declined by 50 percent to 1,645.

With FIRREA, Congress also recognized the importance of fair and accurate appraisals to the real estate industry. With very few exceptions, as of January 1, 1993, every property appraisal in a *federally related* transaction had to be performed by an appraiser licensed or certified by the state in which the property is located. A mortgage loan transaction is federally related when it involves any of the following:

- A federally chartered or insured institution
- Government backing (such as an FHA-insured or VA-guaranteed loan)
- The secondary mortgage market (through which mortgage loans are sold to investors by agencies such as Fannie Mae and Freddie Mac)

As a practical matter, most appraisals must be performed by a state-licensed or certified appraiser. Congress gave the responsibility for establishing appraiser licensing criteria and appraisal standards to the Appraisal Foundation, a private, nonprofit organization whose members include the major appraiser and mortgage brokerage trade associations. The Appraiser Qualifications Board of the Appraisal Foundation sets the minimum level of education and experience that must be required by the states for appraiser licensing. The Uniform Standards of Professional Appraisal Practice (USPAP), created and frequently updated by the Appraisal Standards Board of the Appraisal Foundation, sets out the minimum requirements that appraisals must meet.

Current Licensing Requirements

The minimum requirements for appraiser licensing that took effect in 1993 have been bolstered over the years to increase the required hours of appraiser education as well as the hours of experience necessary for each stage of licensing. Current criteria appear in Figure 1.1. Each state must meet or exceed these requirements for the two levels of certified real property appraiser.

An appraiser trainee may work only under a supervising appraiser and may perform appraisals of only those properties the supervisor is authorized to appraise. The supervising appraiser may supervise only trainees at a time. A licensed real property appraiser may appraise property consisting of the following:

- Non-complex one-to-four residential units having a transaction value less than $1 million
- Complex one-to-four residential units having a transaction value less than $250,000

Figure 1.1 Minimum Appraiser Licensing Requirements

	Education	Experience	Continuing Education
Appraiser Trainee	75 hours, including the 15-hour National USPAP Course	Direct supervision by a supervising appraiser who is in good standing as a state licensed or certified appraiser	14 hours for each year preceding renewal
Licensed Real Property Appraiser	150 hours, including the 15-hour National USPAP Course	2,000 hours of appraisal experience	14 hours for each year preceding renewal; 7-hour National USPAP Update Course at least once every two years
Certified Residential Real Property Appraiser	200 hours (including the 15-hour National USPAP Course) and an AA degree or 21 semester hours of specified courses	2,500 hours of appraisal experience acquired in no fewer than 24 months	14 hours for each year preceding renewal; 7-hour National USPAP Update Course at least once every two years
Certified General Real Property Appraiser	300 hours (including the 15-hour National USPAP Course) and a BA or higher degree or 30 semester hours of specified courses	3,000 hours of appraisal experience acquired in no fewer than 30 months	14 hours for each year preceding renewal; 7-hour National USPAP Update Course at least once every two years

A certified residential real property appraiser may appraise residential property without regard to transaction value or complexity. A certified general real property appraiser may appraise all types of real property.

The discussion here has been very abbreviated. If you want to know more, you will find a detailed chronology of the savings and loan crisis and its aftermath at *www.fdic.gov/bank/historical/s&l*. It is interesting reading for those who experienced that time and a cautionary tale for those who did not. Information about the appraisal industry is available at the Web site of the Appraisal Foundation at *www.appraisalfoundation.org* as well as at the Web site of the Appraisal Institute, *www.appraisalinstitute.org*, the largest trade association of appraisers.

The Appraiser's Role

To produce an appraisal that is as accurate as possible, the appraiser must compile all relevant data, assemble it in an orderly manner, and use procedures and techniques recognized by USPAP to form an opinion of value. Thus, an appraisal is a combination of fact-findings and the appraiser's judgment based on past experience.

In every real estate transaction, the appraiser should act as a disinterested third party. The appraiser's compensation should never be contingent on the determination of value. With no financial interest in the property and nothing to gain or lose from the outcome of the appraisal, the appraiser should be able to objectively evaluate the property's relative merits, appeal, and value.

Of course, appraisers are subject to the same economic factors that impact everyone else. Competition for appraisal work may make some appraisers cut corners or bow to undue influence by the client. Lenders have been known to "shop" for an appraiser who is willing to produce an appraisal that conforms to a transaction price. Appraisers are routinely told the purchase price on which a transaction is based, rather than being allowed to derive an opinion of value that is unaffected, consciously or subconsciously, by the negotiation of the parties.

The public sector isn't immune from outside influences, either. The county tax assessor knows that the income necessary to support his or her department, as well as other public services, will come from the ad valorem (according to value) taxes that are based on assessed valuations. Property taxes form the backbone for financing of government services at the local level, and the public sector tends to thrive when it receives more money—not less.

Despite the pressures that prove irresistible to some appraisers, it is in the ultimate best interest of the appraiser's client to receive as accurate an opinion of value as possible.

The rest of this chapter looks at some of the real estate concepts that help define the property that the appraiser is asked to evaluate.

LAND VERSUS SITE

Land is commonly thought of as the ground or soil. From a real estate standpoint, however, land refers to the earth's surface and everything under or on it and, within limitations, the right to use the airspace above it.

A **site** is land that has been improved to make it ready for the construction of a house, apartment building, shopping mall, or other structure. Improving land for a site may include any of the following:

- Clearing trees, brush, and other vegetation
- Grading the soil to prepare it for construction
- Landscaping the property
- Installing drainage systems for irrigation and storm water runoff
- Providing sewers for waste water
- Making utility connections (water, gas, electricity, cable)
- Putting in sidewalks
- Finishing streets with curbs
- Providing streetlights
- Providing access to roads

Although it appears at the end of the list, road access is perhaps the most essential element to make vacant property suitable for building. Without a road to make it possible to travel to and from the property, it will have virtually no utility as a site.

Figure 1.2 can be used to note the features of a site.

Figure 1.2 Site Features

	YES	NO
Landscaping	_____	_____
Drainage systems	_____	_____
Water	_____	_____
Gas	_____	_____
Electricity	_____	_____
Sidewalks	_____	_____
Curbs	_____	_____
Sewers	_____	_____
Streetlights	_____	_____
Access to roads	_____	_____
_____	_____	_____
_____	_____	_____
_____	_____	_____

REAL ESTATE AND REAL PROPERTY

There is an important distinction between the terms *real estate* and *real property*:

- **Real estate** refers to the physical, tangible land and all things permanently attached to it, which are called **fixtures.**

- **Real property** refers to the rights of ownership of the physical real estate—often called the **bundle of rights.** Included in the bundle are the rights to use, sell, rent, or give away the real estate, as well as to choose *not* to exercise any of those rights.

An individual doesn't actually move or transfer the real estate itself—the dirt, landscaping, and buildings. It is the bundle of rights inherent in the ownership of real estate that are bought and sold in a real estate transaction.

Although the concepts are different, the terms *real estate* and *real property* are often used interchangeably. In some states, such as California, the terms are considered synonymous.

PUBLIC RESTRICTIONS ON LAND USE

About 30 percent of the land in the United States is in public ownership by the federal government, and additional land is owned by the states and local governments (cities or counties). The rest is owned privately by individuals and companies. The government reserves the following four basic powers over the private ownership of real estate:

1. *Taxation.* This is the power to tax real estate to support government functions and sell the property if taxes are not paid.

2. *Eminent domain.* This is the power to take private property for public or private use, provided just compensation is paid. **Eminent domain** has been the subject of much debate in the past few years, following the U.S. Supreme Court's decision in the *Keho* case. In that Connecticut case, the Court decided that private property could be taken for commercial development—a different private use. Some states have passed new laws to make it clear that private property within the state can be taken by a public entity only for a public use.

3. *Police power.* This allows government the right to establish building codes, zoning ordinances, traffic regulations, and other measures that restrict the use of real estate in order to protect the health, safety, morals, and general welfare of the public. There has been a trend toward standardization

of minimum building requirements. The International Building Code, created by the International Codes Council in 2004, has replaced a variety of regional and municipal building codes. In most states, there is a state-wide building code in effect for areas that are not subject to a municipal or county building code. To ensure that structures conform to the allowed zoning and required building specifications, the building code requires a permit for all phases of new construction, starting with grading of the land, with frequent inspections and approvals by a building code official before work can proceed to the next stage.

4. *Escheat.* **Escheat** provides the power to have property ownership transferred to the state if the owner dies leaving no locatable heirs. The state will usually take ownership for only a specific period—say, five years—before selling the property in the event that no heirs are found.

Public restrictions aren't the only limitations placed on how you can use your land. Private restrictions on land use are discussed next.

PRIVATE RESTRICTIONS ON LAND USE

Limitations on how you can use your land may be found in the deed you receive, or you may agree to a use of your land with certain limits.

Deed restrictions are usually found in the deeds to owners of properties that are part of a subdivision development. The restrictions are placed in the deeds by the developer of the land, but benefit the other property owners in the subdivision. By maintaining specific property standards, deed restrictions serve some of the same functions as zoning and building codes. By purchasing the property and accepting the deed containing the restrictions, the buyer agrees to their terms. It is not uncommon for the members of a subdivision to vote on the inclusion of a new provision in the deeds for their properties. Deed restrictions normally relate to the following:

- Type of building
- Land use
- Type of construction
- Building materials
- Building height, setbacks, and square footage
- Cost

Sometimes, deed restrictions are unenforceable because they violate a law or public policy. Racially restrictive covenants found in deeds issued before the 1950s are unenforceable because they are illegal. In an area of high fire risk, a requirement that every structure have a wood shake roof would be unenforceable as a practical matter; even if a local ordinance did not require immediate replacement of such a roof with one that is flame-retardant, a homeowner could hardly be prohibited from doing so.

An **easement** is the right that a property owner provides to others to travel over or use the property. The owner of a lake lot, for example, may grant an easement so that the owner of an adjacent lot can have lake access. An easement may come with the property; for example, a property owner may be prohibited from building on any part of the property that provides access to utility installations. Any easements that burden or benefit a property will be included in the property's legal description.

PERSONAL PROPERTY

Appraisers also must differentiate between real estate and personal property. **Personal property** refers to tangible items that are not permanently attached to or part of the real estate. Items of personal property are not considered fixtures to the real estate. To determine whether an item should be considered personal property or real estate, appraisers and the courts generally consider the following two factors:

1. How the item is attached (whether it can be removed easily)
2. The intent of the person who attached it (to leave the item permanently or to remove it at some future date)

In general, an item remains personal property if it can be removed without serious injury either to the real estate or to the item itself.

Example

A window air conditioner would ordinarily be considered personal property, but if a hole were cut in a wall expressly for the installation of the air conditioner, the unit would probably be considered part of the real estate—a fixture.

Items of personal property are not usually included in a real estate appraisal. The buyer and seller in a sales transaction should agree on the items that are to be included in the sale of the real estate and list those in the purchase contract.

Example

The Morales family inherited a beautiful crystal chandelier, which now hangs in their dining room. When they sell the house, they intend to take the chandelier with them. When it comes time to sell the house, they should make sure that any prospective buyer is aware that the chandelier will be removed before the property is transferred to the new owner.

If litigation is necessary because it is unclear whether an item is a fixture or personal property, the courts will generally favor the buyer over the seller in a sales transaction, and the lender over the borrower in a loan transaction.

A property seller should draw up a list of all personal property items and fixtures in the home. To avoid misunderstandings later on, both the buyer and seller should initial each item to indicate agreement. Figure 1.3 is a form that can be used to list items to be considered personal property and those to be considered fixtures, with a space for the seller or buyer to indicate their agreement to that treatment. There is also room at the bottom of the form to list items that will be subject to negotiation by the parties.

Figure 1.3 Inventory of Personal Property and Fixtures

Personal Property	Agreement
_____	_____ _____
_____	_____ _____
_____	_____ _____
_____	_____ _____
_____	_____ _____
_____	_____ _____
_____	_____ _____

Fixtures — Agreement

Fixtures	Agreement
_____	_____ _____
_____	_____ _____
_____	_____ _____
_____	_____ _____
_____	_____ _____
_____	_____ _____
_____	_____ _____

Items to be negotiated

_____	_____ _____
_____	_____ _____
_____	_____ _____

The Real Estate Marketplace

A market exists when something is for sale and someone wants to buy it. There is a market for real estate just as there is a market for food, clothing, electronics, automobiles, and stocks. The unique feature of the real estate market, of course, is that real estate is *immobile*, making it the one commodity that is truly local. If there is a shortage of housing in Nashville, an oversupply of new homes in Denver won't accommodate the buyers in the Nashville market.

All real estate appraisals are based on information obtained by observing what is happening in the marketplace. The real estate appraised may be a home, commercial property, public-use property (a school or hospital), vacant lot, agricultural land, conservation area, or other property. Whatever its current use and ownership, the probable value of a parcel of real estate will be affected by the local and regional economy, although it will also be affected to some extent by national and even international conditions. Population changes, government fiscal policies, business and industry trends, inflation, interest rates, and the types of loans currently available all have a bearing on the value of real estate. Most important in an appraisal of residential property is a comprehensive analysis of the neighborhood in which the property is located.

This chapter looks at the factors that define and influence the real estate marketplace.

RECENT HISTORY

In the United States, the market for real estate in the post–World War II era has benefited from record high levels of demand and resulting price increases for both new and existing homes and commercial properties. What goes up can come down, however, as every economist and most homeowners can verify. When tracking property values, every decade seems to have a peak and a trough, even though some areas tend to have more extremes than others, with higher highs and lower lows.

In the past decade, housing has alternately been seen as a refuge from the stock market and an even less reliable investment owing to its illiquid nature. A publicly traded stock has the ultimate liquidity; it can be sold when desired—even if the selling price is not the one that was anticipated when the stock was purchased.

A home, on the other hand, typically can be sold only if a number of factors converge:

- A willing buyer with the financial ability to purchase makes an offer that the seller is willing to accept.
- The property fulfills the expectations of the buyer following its close inspection by an experienced home inspector.
- A lender is willing to loan the buyer the funds needed to make the purchase, based on the buyer's income and credit history.
- An appraiser's determination of a property value satisfies the lender's need for an assurance that the property value supports the loan amount.

In the dot-com boom and bust of the 1990s, many investors were burned by the poor performance of stocks that were sold based on promises rather than proven financial results. Fleeing from the stock market, they sought the protection of the only investment that has both a quantifiable use and limited supply: real estate. Record low interest rates helped fuel the growth in residential real estate sales and prices until the exuberance of buyers, developers, and lenders finally hit the brick wall of what has been a growing, but not unlimited, demand for homes. Then, investors who purchased multiple properties (condominiums, in particular) in such desirable metropolitan areas as Miami, Florida, and Las Vegas, Nevada, found that the buyers weren't there. Even worse, some homeowners who purchased at the height of the buying frenzy have found that, a year or two later, their resale opportunities have been limited by the availability of new developments that attract buyers by offering equivalent amenities in new structures at more affordable prices.

Added to the problem of too many homes and not enough buyers has been the fallout of the latest stumbling block for the lending industry—the subprime mortgage crisis. The subprime mortgage crisis is worth some discussion.

THE SUBPRIME MORTGAGE CRISIS

Few homebuyers just entering the real estate marketplace can afford to pay all cash for property. The tax advantages of home ownership can make an all-cash purchase a poor choice in any event. As a result, the cost of credit is a major factor affecting the home purchase decision. Home affordability—the amount of the monthly loan payment—will be determined by the down payment required, the loan amount, the length of the loan term, and the interest rate charged.

Lenders rate a borrower according to the borrower's income reliability and history of debt repayment. The availability of credit thus depends on the loan applicant's income and credit history. A consumer's credit history is available from one of the three major credit reporting companies: Equifax (*www.equifax.com*), Experian (*www.experian.com*), and TransUnion (*www.transunion.com*). A consumer is entitled to one free credit report each year, as explained at *www.annualcreditreport.com*.

A loan applicant's credit score is a way of considering the information provided in the credit report. One company that issues credit scores is the Fair Isaac Corporation, which created an algorithm (mathematical factor) that, when applied to a consumer's income and debt history, produces what is known as a **FICO score**. The FICO score is used by a lender to rate the creditworthiness of a prospective borrower—the higher the score, the better. Information about FICO scores and how to improve your score can be found at *www.myfico.com*.

The market for mortgage loans is categorized by the creditworthiness of the borrowers to whom the loans are made, which defines the level of risk that the lender is undertaking. The highest rated borrowers are in the *prime market* and are rated A (the best). The *subprime market* consists of borrowers in the B and C categories. Each of those is further broken down into + (better) and – (not as good) ratings. A borrower rated A+ has the highest rating.

Cheap money (low interest rates) and what seemed like effortlessly increasing equity lured many lenders and borrowers into loans that required little or no verification of income, the "stated income" or "no-doc" loans. Some loans were interest-only, which meant that the borrower made no payment toward the loan principal; others included the option of making a full payment, or deferring payment on some of the interest owed, which was added to the remaining loan balance (negative amortization). So in some cases, borrowers not only failed to pay down the loans, they constantly added to the amount owed.

The run-up in property values caused by the heightened demand for homes and investments lulled many lenders into a false sense of security in the value of the properties used to secure the loans they made. The assumption of continuing years of 20 percent or 25 percent appreciation also proved to be the downfall of property buyers who took on adjustable-rate mortgages at absurdly low initial interest rates with the expectation that they would refinance the loans before a higher rate took effect.

The 2/28 mortgage (since abandoned by many lenders) offered a fixed, low "teaser" rate for two years, to be followed by a jump to the real effective interest rate for the remaining loan term. Facing loan payments that were double or triple the initial payment amount and the reality of other expenses of home ownership, such as property taxes, many homeowners had no recourse but to default on payments and face foreclosure on their properties. In 2007, the markets that had seen the biggest price increases—California, Florida, and Nevada—also saw the greatest number of foreclosures, but all states saw increases in defaults in the subprime market. The prime market was affected as well, because lenders tightened their underwriting requirements across the board.

Even some homeowners who had lived in their homes for many years got swept up in the wave of refinancing and took advantage of the low interest rates, but they found themselves facing insurmountable debts when their mortgages adjusted to reflect current rates and indexes. To lose a home one has owned for a few years is terrible enough, but to lose a home one has owned for 20 years is a crushing blow.

The influx of investment money into residential real estate was a precipitating factor in the downturn of many markets, but an important factor was also the aggressive marketing of dubious loan products by lenders and mortgage brokers. Many states license mortgage brokers, but others do not, and the level of training and education for mortgage brokers is spotty at best. One outcome of the subprime lending crisis is likely to be regulation of mortgage brokers, including licensing and education requirements. This is similar to what was undertaken with respect to appraisers following the savings and loan crisis of the 1980s, which was discussed in the previous chapter.

MARKET VALUE

This book has already mentioned market value several times, but what exactly is market value?

Market value is the most probable price a buyer is willing to pay a seller for a product on the open market in an arm's-length transaction. Notice that market value is *not* the highest price possible for the property, but the most likely price the property will command. An arm's-length transaction is one in which the following is true:

- The buyer and seller are not related in any way.
- The product has been on the market for a length of time that is reasonable for products of that type.
- Neither the buyer nor seller is acting under duress.
- There are no financing or other concessions beyond what is customary in the marketplace.

A property's market value is frequently referred to as its fair market value. The two terms—*market value* and *fair market value*—mean the same thing. The concept of fairness has nothing to do with favoring or disfavoring either the seller or buyer or of being "fair" to either the seller or buyer in terms of the seller's or buyer's needs or desires. It simply means that the opinion of value is based on an arm's-length transaction, without unusual influences.

Is market value the same as asking price? Is it the same as offering price? Is it the same as selling price? The two possible answers to all three questions are "maybe" and "sometimes." Asking price is what the seller indicates will be an acceptable offer. Offering price is what a buyer actually offers. Selling price is what the seller and buyer finally agree on. All of these may be different from the property's market value, as determined by an appraiser. It is not difficult to think of some of the reasons why this is true.

Asking Price

A seller is free to set whatever asking price he or she chooses for the home that is for sale. The asking price will often be set higher than the price the seller is willing to accept to allow room for negotiation. Even the price the seller is willing to accept is not necessarily an accurate reflection of the property's market value.

It is usually difficult for a homeseller to be entirely objective about a house to which the seller has devoted years of upkeep. The seller may find it hard to believe that all of the dollars expended in improvements do not necessarily add an equal amount to property value. To compound the problem, the seller may have no idea of the actual sales prices of properties in the area. The seller's information may be limited to the asking prices advertised in the local newspaper's classified ad section or the value estimate provided by a Web site. The seller who distrusts real estate agents may miss out on the valuable service that they perform when conducting a competitive market analysis (CMA) of similar properties in the area that are for sale or have sold recently.

Offering Price

A buyer is free to offer whatever the buyer chooses and will often submit an offer lower than the maximum price he or she is willing to pay to allow room for negotiation. Of course, many factors can affect the negotiation. For example, the buyer may offer the seller a quick closing. Even though the seller is not under any duress to sell, the quick closing (and just-as-quick receipt of the sales proceeds) may tempt the seller to accept an offer that is under his or her ideal price.

Selling Price

By definition, it would seem that selling price should almost always be the same as market value. After all, if the appraiser has performed a thorough and accurate job in forming an opinion of a property's market value, shouldn't the selling price match that value? Unfortunately, far too many factors are at work in the average transaction for an appraiser to be able to form an opinion of market value that will be matched exactly by the property's ultimate selling price.

In some negotiations, the sales price is secondary to other considerations such as the terms of financing or the date of possession. If the seller is willing to offer financing, even if the financing is no lower than the prevailing market rate, the buyer will benefit by not having to pay expensive points and loan fees to a lender. In such a case, the seller may be able to hold out for a slightly higher asking price. If the seller needs a quick closing, as happens frequently when the seller has been transferred out of the area or has already purchased a new home, the buyer will have a stronger negotiating position and the selling price will probably be reduced accordingly.

Of course, competing factors may also be at work. For example, what if the seller, because of a job transfer, is forced to sell in a buyer's market—that is, one in which there are significantly more properties available for sale than buyers available to purchase them? Either factor—the forced sale or the buyer's market—could mean a lower selling price than would otherwise be possible. Together, the seller's need to sell and the inhospitality of the marketplace could result in a selling price well below the property's potential in the hands of another seller in another market climate.

VALUE PRINCIPLES

Economists have identified a number of basic value principles at work in any marketplace for a product or service. The same principles apply to a sale of real estate.

Substitution

An appraiser's work relies heavily on the use of the principle of **substitution.** Property value is influenced by the cost to acquire a comparable property—that is, one that has the same design and construction or functional utility as the property under consideration.

For example, suppose that a house on Block A is listed for sale at $600,000 and a similar house on Block B is listed for sale at $675,000. The house on Block A is likely to sell first because it is cheaper. We are assuming, of course, that the properties are indeed similar—that is, that they are alike in terms of lot dimensions and landscaping, size of home, amenities, upkeep, and other features. The typical suburban subdivision or block of urban row houses usually provides ample opportunity to compare selling and asking prices of comparable homes because there may be few design or construction differences among houses.

We will be referring to the principle of substitution throughout this book, particularly in Chapter 7, "The Sales Comparison Approach."

Highest and Best Use

A property achieves its highest value at its most profitable legally and physically permitted use. Determining a property's **highest and best use** should be a part of every appraisal. An appraisal of vacant land can take into account the entire range of legally possible uses for the property. If there is an existing structure, the cost to remove or remodel the building would have to be considered as well. Existing zoning should be taken into account, as well as the possibility of zoning changes.

The appraiser attempts to identify the economic factors that may make different land uses more profitable at different times. Thus, a study of a property's highest and best use involves an analysis of the community and neighborhood and how they are affected by national, state, and regional market trends, as well as the subject property. The same property's highest and best use may also change, even over a short period. The vacant land that was considered ideal for an office park when commercial space was in short supply may be better suited for apartment development a few years down the road if the commercial market has been overbuilt and housing is in short supply.

A house that is built on property zoned only for single-family residential building represents the property's highest and best use.

Externalities

According to the principle of **externalities,** factors outside a property can influence property value. If mortgage interest rates are relatively high, for example, property values may be lower than they would be if loans at lower interest rates were available. If federal mortgage insurance programs, such as that of the Federal Housing Administration (FHA), make additional funds available for lending and homes are available at prices within FHA's insurance limit, more buyers will be drawn into the market and property values should go up as a result.

Supply and Demand

The single greatest influence on negotiations between buyer and seller will usually be the principle of **supply and demand.** The cost of any property will be affected by the number of other similar properties for sale relative to the number of buyers in the marketplace. If there are few buyers in relation to the number of properties for sale, the seller's bargaining position is effectively reduced. If the situation is reversed and there are few properties for sale relative to the number of buyers seeking to make a purchase, the seller can hold out for the maximum price—or more, if a bidding war ensues.

Balance

A market that is in **balance** will tend to have more properties available for sale than there are buyers. There are always some owners who list their properties for sale merely to test the market. Such owners will refuse to sell for anything less than the full asking price, which may be set unrealistically high. These are the sellers who are willing to wait out the market by keeping their homes listed for as long as necessary, or by taking them off the market and relisting them when, theoretically, market values have risen. There will always be some properties that are overpriced, but the marketplace is the great leveler that ultimately indicates just how much buyers are willing to pay for the privilege of home ownership.

Property uses are said to be in balance when there are a sufficient number of complementary property types; that is, the number of residential units is adequate for the number of commercial and industrial units. A community that has too few retail stores for its population, for instance, will be less desirable than the community that can offer a good mix of shopping for most everyday needs. In addition, the community with too few business establishments will probably suffer from decreased sales tax revenue and other exactions that can help support city services, and residential property owners will pay higher property taxes as a result.

Competition

The effect of the principle of **competition** is evident when home values lower as competition increases (more properties are available on the market). It also is evident when home values rise as competition decreases (fewer properties are available on the market).

On the other hand, increased competition may serve as a benefit or a detriment to a commercial property owner. Retail stores are especially sensitive to the combined forces of the demand for their products and the number of other stores available to supply the demand. At first, competition may be viewed with suspicion as potential customers are lost to another establishment. With enough competition, however, the retail area may become a center of trade and attract even more customers than a single store ever could alone. This phenomenon is commonly exhibited in shopping malls, where merchandisers of similar products benefit from their shared location, particularly when care has been taken to provide an overall diversity of products and services.

Change

Every property is influenced by the principle of **change.** All factors affecting property value, whether physical or economic, are subject to change. The change may be tumultuous, as when earthquakes, fires, or hurricanes wreak disaster on wide areas, or it may be as gradual as the routine wear and tear of the elements. The marketplace, too, undergoes constant change. Interest rates, levels of employment and income, and other factors affecting demand can change with frightening speed. The professional appraiser must keep up with economic trends to be able to predict as accurately as possible their possible effect on the marketplace.

Conformity, Progression, and Regression

Generally, homes reach their highest value only when they are in **conformity** with others in the neighborhood. This means that they should be alike in terms of age, method and quality of construction, design, and amenities. The value of a home that does not conform to others in the neighborhood may actually benefit, if the home is of lesser quality or upkeep than its neighbors. This is an example of the principle of **progression.** The general good appearance of the neighborhood can reflect favorably on a home that is not in as good condition. Likewise, however, the value of a home that would otherwise create a favorable impression will suffer if the rest of the neighborhood is not in as good condition. This is an example of the principle of **regression.**

Growth, Equilibrium, and Decline

Individual properties, like neighborhoods, also undergo constant change. The effects of ordinary physical deterioration and market demand dictate that property will pass through three stages:

1. Growth, when improvements are being built and demand is rising
2. Equilibrium, when the neighborhood is virtually complete and properties appear to undergo little change
3. Decline, when individual properties require increasing amounts of upkeep while demand decreases

High demand for housing and stringent growth controls in many urban areas have resulted in a new fourth stage that could be termed revitalization. Older, neglected neighborhoods that once would have continued to decline have become newly attractive. Many property buyers have decided that the high cost of upkeep of older homes may be worth the convenience of a location close to the downtown business district and cultural center. This process, also described as gentrification, is particularly evident in cities with very high property costs, such as San Francisco.

Anticipation

Usually, one of the reasons real estate is purchased is the expectation that it will increase in value over time. Especially considering the growing cost of real estate relative to personal income, the **anticipation** of the property's future value is an important factor. Certainly, the vast majority of property buyers would like to see some profit earned on their investments through an increase in their equity.

Unfortunately, the recent dramatic inflation in real estate values in many parts of the country may have given some current property owners and sellers a distorted view of the potential for appreciation of their properties. In a period of rapid appreciation, new entrants to the housing marketplace learn to accept the inevitable outcome of increased demand and decreased supply. The "acceptable" percentage of gross income devoted to housing is no longer the 25 percent that homebuyers in the 1950s and 1960s could expect to pay, but a percentage that is one-third or more of gross income. That figure is even more significant when you consider that the income is typically generated by two wage earners.

The principle of anticipation has not been forgotten, of course. Even the newest homeowners typically expect their property to provide them a nice nest egg some day, even if it is accomplished only by their paying down the mortgage.

Contribution

An improvement to real estate can help increase a property's market value. The increase in value, however, will not necessarily be the same as the dollar amount spent on the improvement. An improvement's **contribution** to market value is measured by its effect on the value of the entire property, rather than the intrinsic cost of the improvement.

Some improvements, such as a remodeled basement, will usually not contribute their entire cost to a home's market value. Other improvements, such as a second bathroom, may contribute more than their cost to the home's market value.

Even if the improvement is one that is sought after in the community, the home-owner must guard against making an improvement that is far too luxurious, too expensive, or too personalized for the average buyer's taste and budget.

Many homeowners come to grief because they fail to understand this basic value principle. They don't realize that certain improvements may increase the comfort and utility of their home *for them*, but those improvements may not be considered necessary or even desirable by potential buyers. The wrong improvement or the right improvement poorly executed can even bring down the market value of a home. The suburban home that looks like a turreted castle may fill the heart of its owner/remodeler with joy, but the real estate agent who attempts to sell the property at a price that reflects its cost to the owner will have a frustrating task.

The wrong improvement (in terms of contribution to market value) isn't neces-sarily one of major proportions. Even a fireplace addition, which might ordinar-ily be a dollar-for-dollar contribution in some communities, can be overdesigned or overbuilt far out of proportion to the needs of the typical homeowner. Home remodelers are notorious for changing their minds after a project is under way, without realizing the impact any change can have on construction estimates. The "simple" substitution of imported marble for common used brick can have a sig-nificant effect on both material and labor costs.

Law of Increasing Returns and Law of Decreasing Returns

It is possible to overimprove a property. This happens when so many property improvements have been made that they no longer have any positive effect on value. As long as property improvements create a proportionate or greater increase in value, the **law of increasing returns** is in effect. When additional improve-ments no longer bring a corresponding increase in value, the **law of decreasing returns** is in effect.

Every neighborhood has at least one example of the "tinkerer." This is the homeowner who can't stop working on his or her home. After the bathroom sky-light is installed, it's time to redecorate the living room or remodel the kitchen. When the inside work is finished (temporarily), it's time to regrade the lawn and add a new deck or gazebo. Up to a certain point, all of these improvements can add at least some value to a house. If the property is a real "fixer-upper," the law of decreasing returns may not kick in for quite some time. Eventually, however, the home will be improved beyond the needs and financial capabilities of typical buyers in the market area.

Example: Life in the Fast Lane

Sellers often have unrealistic expectations of what their property is worth. Let's consider an example in light of the value principles you have just read in this chapter.

Cathy Clark is selling her two-bedroom, one-bath condominium in a western suburb of Chicago, Illinois. She purchased the condo in 2002 for $142,000. Since then, she has taken great pains to redecorate each room in great taste, applying expensive wallpaper herself and sanding and refinishing the woodwork and floors. Because her company is moving its headquarters to a far northwestern suburb, Cathy plans to sell her condo and purchase a small, detached house in a new subdivision in McHenry County. In fact, she already has placed a deposit on a model she particularly likes. Cathy gathers all her receipts for materials she used in remodeling her condo, computes a reasonable charge per hour for her labor, and adds the total to her purchase price. She then factors in 10 percent appreciation for each year she has owned the condo, based on a report about price appreciation in the United States that she read recently on the Internet. Finally, she subtracts her purchase price and costs from her estimated appreciated value to determine what her net profit from a sale should be. Her figures look like this:

Purchase Price		$142,000
Materials		
Wallpaper—30 rolls @ $50	$1,500	
Sandpaper	17	
Rental of sander	75	
Varnish	82	
Miscellaneous—wallpaper paste, brushes, cleanup	63	
Labor—105 hours @ $10	1,050	
		$2,787
Total Investment		144,787
After Appreciation for Six Years @ 10 percent		256,499
Net Profit ($256,499 – $144,787)		$111,712

Cathy is very pleased with the results of her calculations and immediately makes an appointment with a nearby real estate broker to discuss listing her property for sale. The broker comes over that evening and begins his presentation. Cathy is a bit restless as the broker discusses the services his company can make available to her. She is puzzled when the broker mentions that he has brought along statistics on recent sales and listings of other condominiums in the area. Cathy is not very happy at all when the broker patiently explains to her why his competitive market analysis indicates that her condominium should bring a sales price somewhere in the $175,000 to $200,000 range.

In this example, Cathy Clark made a couple of assumptions that many homeowners make when they try to value their properties themselves:

1. Cathy assumed that every dollar she invested in improvements to her property—both in materials and time (her labor)—resulted in a dollar-for-dollar increase in the property's value. She never heard of either the principle of contribution or the law of decreasing returns.

2. Cathy assumed that the rate of appreciation on her property has been the same as the overall rate of appreciation of all real estate in the country. She never heard of the principle of substitution or the principle of supply and demand. She has no inkling that externalities can impact her property's value. Because she is not in real estate, she has no interest in the number of other properties similar to her own that would be her competition in the marketplace. On top of everything else, Cathy's condo is in an older building that needs a new roof and tuck-pointing, and several brand-new condominium developments are available in the area at below-market interest rates.

If you were in Cathy's place, you might not be happy with the sales prospects conveyed to you by the real estate agent, but at least you would have some idea of the economic principles behind the agent's analysis.

The Appraisal Worksheet can be used to analyze a home and its neighborhood in terms of some of the valuation principles that have been considered in this chapter.

APPRAISAL WORKSHEET

Is the present use of the property its highest and best use? _____

In general, is the home in better condition, about the same condition, or worse condition than others in the neighborhood? *Explain.*

_____

_____

Does the home conform to others in the neighborhood—	Yes	No
in age?	____	____
in lot size?	____	____
in home size?	____	____
in method and quality of construction?	____	____
in architectural style?	____	____
in interior layout?	____	____
in number of bedrooms?	____	____
in number of bathrooms?	____	____
in kind and maturity of landscaping?	____	____
in outdoor amenities, such as a deck or pool?	____	____

How old is the neighborhood?_____

Is the neighborhood in the stage of growth, equilibrium, decline, or revitalization?_____

What improvements have been made to the home?

_____

_____

Do you think the home is worth more now than when purchased? *Explain.*

_____

_____

The Appraisal Process 3

The basic problem when buying or selling real estate is deciding what it is worth. To derive an opinion of value, the appraiser uses three traditional appraisal methods: the sales comparison approach, the cost approach, and the income capitalization approach.

This chapter focuses on the basic definition of each of the value approaches. Also covered are the steps involved in the appraisal process, from an appraisal assignment through the final opinion of value.

SALES COMPARISON APPROACH

In the **sales comparison approach,** an opinion of value is obtained by comparing the property being appraised—the subject property—to recent sales of similar, nearby properties, called **comparables** or **comps.** The theory is that the value of the subject property is directly related to the sales prices of the comparable properties.

The objective of the sales comparison approach is to form an opinion of the market value of the subject property. As stated previously, market value is the most probable price a property should bring in a sale occurring under normal market conditions—an arm's-length transaction. Market value is based on actual sales of comparable properties. The appraiser must collect, classify, analyze, and interpret a body of market data.

The rationale of the sales comparison approach is that a knowledgeable buyer will not pay more for a property than the cost to acquire a comparable alternative property (principle of substitution).

To implement the sales comparison approach, the appraiser finds three to five or more properties that have been sold recently and are similar to the subject property. The appraiser notes any dissimilar features and makes an adjustment for each by using the following formula:

Sales Price of Comparable Property ± Adjustments
= Indicated Value of Subject Property

Adjustments are made to the sales price of a comparable property by *adding* the value of features present in the subject property but not in the comparable property, and *subtracting* the value of features present in the comparable property but not in the subject property.

The adjusted sales prices of the comparables represent the probable value range of the subject property. From this range, a single market value estimate can be selected.

Major types of adjustments include those made for physical (on-site) features, locational (off-site) influences, conditions of the sale (buyer-seller motivation and financing terms), and the time from the date of the sale.

Here's a rule to remember when making adjustments:

A comparable property is always adjusted (either + or −) to make it as similar to the subject property as possible.

This means that a property that has characteristics *more* valuable than the subject must be adjusted *downward*. A property that has characteristics *less* valuable than the subject must be adjusted *upward*. Let's see how this works.

Example

- House A, the subject property, has central air-conditioning and a garage.
- A comparable property, House B, sold for $300,000 one month before the time of the appraisal. House B has a garage but no central air-conditioning, which is valued at $5,000.
- House C is comparable to the subject and sold recently for $285,000. House C has central air-conditioning but no garage, which is valued at $22,000.
- House D, also comparable to the subject property, sold recently for $330,000. It has both a garage and central air-conditioning. House D, however, is located in a better area of the neighborhood than the subject is, because it backs up to a conservation area. The location adjustment is valued at $20,000.

A summary of the adjustment information is as follows:

Comparable Sales Chart

	Comparables		
	B	C	D
Sales price	$300,000	$285,000	$330,000
Location			− 20,000
Garage		+ 22,000	
Air-conditioning	+ 5,000		
Adjusted sales price	$305,000	$307,000	$310,000

The value of House A, the subject property, will fall within the price range of the adjusted comparable properties—that is, between $305,000 and $310,000. Large differences in value might suggest that the properties are not similar enough. In such cases, the appraiser would have to recheck the characteristics of the comparable properties and the validity of the sales.

The accuracy of an appraisal using the sales comparison approach depends on the appraiser's use of reliable adjustment values. How to determine these values and adjust for property differences is explained more fully in Chapter 7, which is devoted to the sales comparison approach.

COST APPROACH

Using the **cost approach,** the appraiser estimates the present reproduction cost of the house plus any other improvements to the land (such as a garage or patio) as if they were *new.* The appraiser then subtracts any loss in value caused by the depreciation of the improvements. **Depreciation** includes all of the influences that reduce the value of the subject house below its current reproduction cost.

Finally, the appraiser adds the value of the site itself, usually found by analyzing sales of similar vacant sites.

The rationale of the cost approach is that a knowledgeable buyer will pay no more for a house than the cost of constructing a substitute house on a similar lot and in similar condition.

The following formula for the cost approach is:

Cost of Improvements New − Depreciation on Improvements
+ Site Value = Property Value

Depreciation may occur through either deterioration or obsolescence. Deterioration is a loss in value to a home resulting from ordinary wear and tear, disintegration, and exposure to the elements over time. The effects of deterioration may be a worn out roof that needs new shingles, peeling paint, cracked windows, and other physical deficiencies that make the property less desirable to potential buyers. **Obsolescence** can be functional or external. **Functional obsolescence** is a loss in value caused by deficiencies within the property such as poor traffic patterns, outmoded room layout or design, and inadequate mechanical equipment. **External obsolescence** is a loss in value caused by negative conditions outside the property, such as a lack of demand for properties in the neighborhood, changes in zoning or property uses in the area, and the presence of nuisances and hazards such as excessive noise, smoke, and traffic.

Example

The subject house is similar in size, design, and quality of construction to a new house that cost $550,000 to build. The subject house has depreciated by 10 percent due to normal wear and tear and is on a lot valued separately at $140,000. Using the cost approach formula yields the following:

$$\$550,000 - (\$550,000 \times .10) + \$140,000 = \text{Property Value}$$
$$\$550,000 - \$55,000 + \$140,000 = \$635,000$$

The indicated value of the subject property is $635,000.

INCOME CAPITALIZATION APPROACH

The **income capitalization approach** is an analysis based on the relationship between the rate of return that an investor or buyer expects or requires and the net income that a property produces. This approach is used primarily for valuing income-producing properties such as apartment buildings, shopping centers, and office buildings.

When applying the income capitalization approach to value, an appraiser must develop an operating statement for the property being appraised. This can be accomplished in five basic steps:

1. Estimate the potential gross income (rent plus all other income earned by the property).
2. Deduct an allowance for vacancies and collection losses (usually estimated as a percentage of potential gross income).

3. Calculate the amount of effective gross income (potential gross income less vacancy and collection losses).

4. Estimate the operating expenses.

5. Deduct the expenses from the effective gross income to obtain the net operating income from the subject property.

Once a property's net operating income is known, the appraiser must develop the buyer's required rate of investment return. This rate of return is called the **capitalization rate** and is determined by comparing the relationship of the net operating income to the sales price of similar properties that have been sold in the current market.

Thus, value can be computed by using the following formula:

$$\frac{\text{Net Operating Income}}{\text{Capitalization Rate}} = \text{Property Value}$$

Example

A buyer requires a 10 percent return on an apartment building that produces a net operating income of $150,000 per year. Applying the income capitalization approach formula, the property value is $150,000 ÷ .10, or $1,500,000.

Obviously, the income capitalization approach can be the most technically complex method of appraisal when applied to large income-producing properties. To perform such appraisals, an understanding of gross and net income streams, tax rules, and capitalization techniques is essential. These concepts, however, are beyond the scope of this book. When appraising single-family homes, a far simpler method can be used as an alternative to the income capitalization approach. This method is based on the assumption that value is related to the market rent the property can be expected to earn.

Market rent is the rental income that a property would most likely command on the open market as indicated by current rents paid for comparable space. To find the market rent, you must know what rent tenants have paid and are currently paying on comparable properties. By comparing present and past performances of properties similar to the subject, you should be able to determine the subject property's rent potential. By analyzing sales prices of comparable properties, you can determine the factor, or **gross rent multiplier (GRM),** that represents the relationship between market rent and market value. When the appropriate GRM is applied to the rental income the subject property is expected to produce, the result is an indication of market value. When appraising single-family residences, a rent multiplier is an accepted tool in the income capitalization approach to value.

The gross rent multiplier is a number that expresses the relationship between the sales price of a residential property and its gross monthly unfurnished rental. This ratio can be expressed by the following formula:

$$\frac{\text{Sales Price}}{\text{Gross Rent}} = \text{GRM}$$

To establish a reasonably accurate GRM, you should obtain recent sales and rental data from five or more properties similar to the subject that have sold in the same market area and were rented at the time of sale.

Figure 3.1 illustrates the calculation of a monthly GRM.

Figure 3.1 Gross Rent Multiplier Calculation

Sale No.	Sales Price	Monthly Rental	Gross Rent Multiplier
1	$190,000	$950	200.00
2	185,000	890	207.87
3	187,000	915	204.37
4	195,000	980	198.98
5	189,000	930	203.23
		Average =	202.89

Based on this marketing analysis, the appraiser probably would use 203 as the GRM.

The estimated GRM can then be applied to the projected rental of the subject property to arrive at an opinion of market value. This can be found using the following formula:

$$\text{Gross Rent} \times \text{GRM} = \text{Market Value}$$

Example

An appraiser has determined that the market rent for the subject property is $950 per month. The range of GRMs derived from recent sales of comparable properties is from 150 to 160. The appraiser concludes that the subject property's GRM should be 155. Using the GRM formula results in the following:

$$\$950 \times 155 = \$147,250$$

The indicated value of the subject property using the gross rent multiplier method is $147,250.

RELATIONSHIP OF APPROACHES

All three approaches to value are market-oriented and must reflect market data and the market behavior of buyers (and builders, in the case of the cost approach).

Using the sales comparison approach, the subject property is compared with other similar properties recently sold, and adjustments are made for any differences. The prices at which properties sell in the market indicate the reactions of typical investors and users.

The income capitalization approach analyzes market-determined rents and expenses. The approach is based on the assumption that an investor in income property expects a certain return on the investment. On the basis of that return, the investor decides what to buy and how much to pay. For single-family houses, gross monthly rental is used and the ratio derived is the gross rent multiplier.

With the cost approach, an opinion of value is obtained by adding land value to estimated reproduction cost new, less depreciation of the improvements. Land value is determined by comparing the subject land with similar land recently sold in the market. Features of vacant land might include installation of utilities, composition of soil, terrain, shape, zoning, and favorable location.

All the elements of cost are market phenomena, as are all types of depreciation. The estimate of reproduction cost new, for example, must be based on current labor rates and material costs. Physical deterioration is measured by the cost of labor and materials needed to cure it. Functional and external obsolescence are measured by the behavior of typical buyers, because their reactions to style, function, utility of buildings, and the like give a reliable indication of the amount of loss incurred.

As a general rule, the sales comparison approach is most useful when appraising single-family homes, and this is the approach that is required for all federally related residential appraisals. The cost approach is best applied to appraising non-income-producing property, such as museums, libraries, churches, schools, and other institutional buildings, where there is no income and few sales, if any. The income capitalization approach is most useful when appraising investment property.

For any formal appraisal assignment, all three approaches can and should be used whenever possible. If nothing else, each approach serves as a check against the others. Keep in mind, however, that each approach must be based on verified market data.

STEPS IN THE APPRAISAL PROCESS

The flowchart in Figure 3.2 outlines the steps by which an appraisal is carried out. The basic process is generally the same, regardless of the purpose of the appraisal and the type of property being appraised, and it follows these eight steps:

1. *Identify the problem.* The appraiser begins by identifying the subject property—by its mailing address and by its more precise legal description, which can be found on an existing deed, mortgage instrument, title policy, or various other public records.

    The appraiser then must note what the appraisal is to accomplish. Most often, the appraisal will be conducted to determine the market value for a prospective sale or loan. What will be the effective date of the appraisal? Most appraisals call for a current opinion of value—date near or on the day the property is inspected. In some cases, a valuation as of a date in the past or future is required. Once the objectives or goals of the appraisal are known, the approach(es) best suited to the subject property can be selected. All three basic approaches are traditionally used by appraisers whenever possible. Each method serves as a check against the others and narrows the range within which the final opinion of value will fall. Occasionally, only one approach will be appropriate, because only a limited amount of data will be available for some properties.

2. *Determine the scope of work.* Based on the value approaches to be used, the appraiser determines the kinds of data that must be collected and the sources of that data.

3. *Gather, record, and verify the necessary data.* Five categories of data are needed to make a reliable estimate of value:

    - General data on the geographic and economic features of the nation, region, city, and neighborhood
    - Specific data on the subject site and improvements—including a detailed physical description
    - Sales data on comparable properties—to apply the sales comparison approach
    - Cost data on construction of a like property plus accrued depreciation data on the subject property—to apply the cost approach
    - Sales and income data from properties similar to the subject that have been sold in the same market area and were rented at the time of the

sale—to apply the gross rent multiplier method, a form of income approach for residential properties

The type of property being appraised will dictate the kinds of data that must be collected.

4. *Analyze data.* The appraiser analyzes and interprets the market forces that influence the subject property and determines the property's most profitable use on which to base the final opinion of value. For most residential subdivision developments, the current use of the property is its highest and best use.

5. *Form an opinion of land value.* The location and improvements of the subject site (except for structures) are compared to those of similar nearby sites that have been sold recently. Adjustments are made for significant differences. The adjusted prices of the properties most like the subject are used to form an opinion of value of the subject site.

6. *Form an opinion of value using each of the three approaches.* Using the sales comparison approach, the sales prices of recently sold comparable properties are adjusted to derive a value for the subject property. With the cost approach, the cost of property improvements less depreciation on improvements is added to the site value. Applying the income capitalization approach, value is based on the rental income the property is capable of earning, and in the simplest application of the income capitalization approach, a gross rent multiplier is derived.

7. *Reconcile values for a final opinion of value.* All information must be reconciled or correlated and conclusions drawn from the collected facts. The appraiser never simply averages differing value opinions. The most relevant approach, based on analysis and judgment, receives the greatest weight when determining the market value of the subject property.

8. *Report the final opinion of value.* The appraiser's conclusion of value is presented in the form requested by the client. The report should include a summary of the data analyzed, the methods used, and the reasoning that led to the appraiser's conclusion.

Figure 3.2 The Appraisal Process

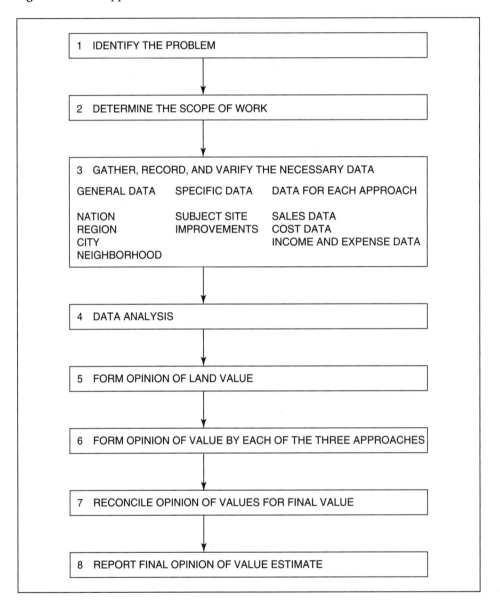

SUMMARY

The sales comparison approach is generally the best method for finding the fair market value of a house. The income capitalization approach is the least reliable, while the cost approach requires up-to-date information on current construction costs as well as intricate methods of depreciating older houses. Regardless of what approach is used, however, one must remember that the fair market value of any house is greatly influenced by what the owner is willing to sell it for and by what the buyer is willing to pay for it. This final agreed-on price in a specific transaction is, for all practical purposes, the value of the property.

The appraisal process begins by identifying the problem, that is, the purpose of the appraisal. By gathering, recording, and verifying all the necessary data, then analyzing and interpreting that information, the appraiser can form an opinion of value based on knowledge and understanding, and not on guesswork.

In the Appraisal Worksheet that follows is a list of questions to help you gather some preliminary facts about the market picture in a neighborhood. You can find the answers to these questions by talking to local real estate agents and builders and consulting a variety of Internet resources, such as the Web sites of the local and state associations of REALTORS®.

APPRAISAL WORKSHEET

1. Is the population in the area growing? Declining? Holding steady? _____

2. How many new houses are for sale and how fast are they selling? _____

3. How many existing (preowned) houses are for sale and how fast are they selling?_____

4. What kinds of houses are selling best and why?_____
   _____

5. What kinds of houses aren't selling well? Why?_____
   _____

6. How great is the demand for rental housing?_____

7. What do homes rent for per month? Range_____

8. Is there a standard gross rent multiplier used in the area? If so, what is it?_____

9. What locations in the area are selling well?_____
   _____

10. What special features are liked and disliked by house hunters?_____
    _____

11. What is the cost per square foot for homes in the area?_____

12. What is the price range of homes sold in each market?

    New_____

    Existing_____

    Rental_____

Data Collection and the Data Bank

4

At every step in the appraisal process, an appraiser will make use of data that has been diligently collected and carefully analyzed for its applicability to the property being appraised. The kinds of data the appraiser collects and considers are discussed in this chapter. Even though you may not have the resources of a professional appraiser, you should be able to find at least some of the data that will be mentioned. The more data you can find and interpret, the better you will understand the economic forces that affect property value.

THE APPRAISAL PROCESS

The last chapter covered the steps in the appraisal process, which are illustrated in the flowchart that appears on page 38. As the chart indicates, a considerable amount of data must be collected to form an accurate opinion of value. The appraiser will need the following information:

- General data on the nation, region, city, and neighborhood
- Specific data on the subject site and improvements
- Sales data for the sales comparison approach
- Cost and depreciation data for the cost approach
- Income and expense data for the income approach

The appraiser also must keep in mind the type of property being appraised. Certain data will be more important for some types of property and thus will receive more emphasis in the appraiser's research. Sales data on recent sales of comparable properties will be especially important when appraising a single-family residence, for example. Income and expense data will be of greatest importance when appraising an investment property, such as an apartment or office building. For special-purpose properties, such as school buildings, data on building costs tends to be most important.

THE DATA BANK

Figure 4.1 is the Data Bank. You will be referring to it throughout the rest of this book to help you determine the types of information required for an appraisal and where the information can be found.

The Source List

The first part of the Data Bank lists the typical sources that supply the information required for a real estate appraisal. Not every source listed may be available to you, and there may be other sources not on the list that are unique to your community. You can add to the list in the spaces numbered 45 through 50. Many of the sources have websites that provide a convenient way to access updated information.

Figure 4.1 Data Bank

Data Source List	
1. Personal inspection	18. Local chamber of commerce
2. Seller	19. Property managers or owners
3. Buyer	20. Building and architectural plans
4. Broker	21. Accountants
5. Salesperson	22. Financial statements
6. Neighbors	23. Building architects, contractors, and engineers
7. County register of deeds	
8. Recorded mortgages and other financing instruments	24. County or city engineering commission
9. Title reports	25. Regional or county government officials
10. Transfer maps or books	
11. Recorded subdivision plat maps	26. Area planning commissions
12. Area maps (topographic, soil)	27. Highway commissioner's office, road commission
13. Recorded leases	
14. Banks and other lending institutions	28. Newspaper advertisements
15. City hall or county courthouse	29. Multiple listing systems
16. Assessor's office	30. Cost manuals (state, local, private)
17. Published information on transfers, leases, or assessed valuation	31. Local material suppliers

(Continued)

32. Public utility companies

33. United States Bureau of the Census

34. Department of Commerce

35. Federal Housing Administration

36. Government councils

37. Local association of REALTORS®

38. National, state, or local association of home builders

39. Public transportation officials

40. Professional journals

41. Railroad and transit authorities or companies

42. Labor organizations

43. Employment agencies

44. Airlines and bus lines, moving companies

45.

46.

47.

48.

49.

50.

A. Regional Data

Types of Information	Sources
Topography	12
Natural resources	18, 12
Climate	18
Public transportation:	
Air	18, 44
Rail	18, 41
Expressways	27, 12
Population trends	26, 33, 36
Political organization and policies	25
Employment level	36, 42
Level of business activity and growth	14, 18
Average family income	26, 18
New building (amount and kind)	34
Percentage of home ownership	33
Electrical power consumption and new hookups	32

B. City Data

Types of Information	Sources
Topography	1, 12
Natural resources	1, 12
Climate	18
Public transportation:	
Air	18, 44

(*Continued*)

Rail	41, 44
Bus	39, 44
Subway	39, 44
Expressways	27, 12
Traffic patterns	15, 24, 27
Population trends	26, 33, 36
Family size	26
Zoning	15, 26
Building codes	15, 23, 24
Political organization, policies, and personnel	15
Employment level	18, 36, 42
Professions, trades, or skills required	18
Level of business activity and growth	14, 18
Average family income	18, 26
Rental rates	19, 37
Percentage of vacancies	4, 35, 37
New building (amount and kind)	19, 37, 38
Building permits issued	15, 24
Bank deposits and loans	14, 18
Percentage of home ownership	4, 33, 37
Tax structure	15, 16
Electrical power consumption and new hookups	32

C. Neighborhood Data

Types of Information	*Sources*
Topography	1, 12
Boundaries	1, 4, 15, 11
Public transportation:	
Bus	39
Subway	39
Frequency of service	39
Distance to boarding point	1, 39
Distance and time to reach central business district	1, 39
Traffic patterns	1, 26, 36, 39
Family size	4, 26

(*Continued*)

Population density	18, 26
Population trend	18, 36
Zoning, codes, or regulations	15, 24, 26
Employment level	4, 14, 18
Professions and trades	4, 6, 18
Average family income	33, 34, 18, 42
Percentage of home ownership	14, 37, 33
Level of business activity and growth	14, 18
New building (amount and kind)	23, 31
Building permits issued	15, 24
Taxes and assessments	15, 16
Utilities or improvements available (streets, curbs, sidewalks; water; electricity; telephone; gas; sewers)	15, 32
Percent built up	15, 37
Predominant type of building	1, 16, 19, 23
Typical age of buildings	1, 16, 19, 23
Condition of buildings	1, 26, 36, 31
Price range of typical properties	4, 9, 35, 37
Marketability	4, 37
Life cycle	1, 4
Land value trend	4, 16, 37
Location of facilities:	
Churches	1, 26, 12
Schools	1, 26, 44
Shopping	1, 26, 44
Recreational, cultural	1, 26, 44
Avenues of approach	1, 24
Types of services offered	32
Availability of personnel	26, 18
Employee amenities (shopping, dining, banking facilities)	1
Marketing area	26, 18
Competition	1, 18
Types of industry (light, heavy)	18
Sources of raw materials	18
Hazards and nuisances	1, 6, 25

(Continued)

Deed restrictions	7, 9
Changing use of area	4, 18

D. Site Data

Types of Information	Sources
Legal description	7
Dimensions and area	1, 7, 11
Street frontage	1, 7, 11
Location in block	7, 11
Topography	7, 12
Topsoil and drainage	23, 12
Landscaping	1
Improvements:	
Streets, curbs, sidewalks	1, 15, 24
Water	32
Electricity	32
Telephone	32
Gas	32
Sewers	1, 15, 24
Tax rates and assessed valuation	16
Liens and special assessments	9, 16
Zoning, codes, or regulations	16, 26
Easements and encroachments	1, 7, 9
Status of title	9

E. Building Data

Types of Information	Sources
Architectural style	1, 23
Date of construction and additions	7, 16, 24
Placement of building on land	1, 24, 12
Dimensions and floor area	20, 11
Floor plan(s)	20, 24
Construction materials used (exterior and interior)	20, 23, 31
Utilities available	1, 32, 18
Interior utility and other installations:	1, 16, 20
Heating and air-conditioning	
Plumbing	

(Continued)

Wiring

Special equipment, such as elevators

Exceptions to zoning, codes, or regulations	7, 24, 26
Status of title	9
Mortgages and liens	7, 14
Condition of building	1, 16, 26

F. Sales Data

Types of Information	Sources
Date of sale	1 to 7, 29
Sales price	1 to 7, 29
Name of buyer and seller	1 to 7, 29
Deed book and page	7, 10
Reasons for sale and purchase	2 to 5

G. Cost Data

Types of Information	Sources
Building reproduction cost	23, 30, 31, 42
Building replacement cost	23, 30, 31, 42
Depreciation factors:	
Physical deterioration	1, 23, 30
Functional obsolescence	1, 20, 23, 30
External obsolescence	1, 23, 26, 30

H. Income and Expense Data

Types of Information	Sources
Income data (both subject and comparable properties):	
Annual income	22
Current lease terms	1, 19
Occupancy history	19, 22
Collection loss history	19, 22
Fixed expense data (both subject and comparable properties):	16, 19, 22, 40
Real estate taxes	
Insurance	
Operating expense data (both subject and comparable properties):	16, 19, 22, 40
Management	

(Continued)

Payroll	
Legal and accounting	
Maintenance	
Repairs	
Supplies	
Painting and decorating	
Fuel	
Electricity	
Miscellaneous	
Reserves for replacement	1, 22, 30

Types of Data Needed

The Data Bank contains eight lists that indicate the most appropriate sources for the various types of data necessary at every step in the appraisal process. Each type of listed information is keyed to one or more of the 44 sources of information itemized in the source list. You can add references to any other sources that you have found useful. Here's how the Data Bank works.

Example

A new subdivision is being built not far from your home. During a Sunday drive, you notice that construction work has begun along both sides of the roadway, but no workers are present whom you can question. How can you find out what kind of work is under way?

In Data Bank List D, "Site Data," you look up "Improvements" and find four possible sources of information—source list numbers 1, 15, 24, and 32. The sources are (1) personal inspection, (15) city hall or county courthouse, (24) county or city engineering commission, and (32) public utility companies. Because you already have inspected the property personally, you would contact the other sources, the most pertinent one first. In this case, the county or city engineering commission could probably tell you the reason for the construction activity. There may be a Web site on which announcements of construction activity are posted. If the activity involves a private project, the department that issues building permits should have the information that you want.

DATA FORMS

As with any other project that requires the collection of a great deal of information, using well-drafted forms can help an appraisal proceed much more smoothly, efficiently, and accurately. Completing data collection forms can help ensure that no details of the property, its location, or the information required for each of the three appraisal techniques are overlooked.

The rest of this chapter includes forms that can be used to collect and record data on the neighborhood, site, and building that are the subject of an appraisal. These are the types of information that will be most readily available to you and are the easiest to understand. A professional appraiser would also have considerable information on the region and city and would have to update that information frequently. Part of an appraiser's job is to keep up to date on economic indicators, such as employment level and business starts (or failures), as well as political trends that could signal governmental policy changes affecting property values. The more aware you make yourself of wider economic influences, the better you will be able to identify and understand the factors that affect the value of a property.

Neighborhood Data Form

A Neighborhood Data Form, such as the one shown in Figure 4.2, can help an appraiser gather some of the basic information needed for an appraisal report. An appraiser who makes many appraisals in the same area would probably not have to complete a new Neighborhood Data Form for each appraisal. The appraiser would have to update the form as often as necessary, perhaps only every year or perhaps more often, as current economic conditions dictated.

Although Data Bank List C, "Neighborhood Data," supplies sources for much of the needed neighborhood information, a considerable amount of fieldwork is still necessary. The appraiser must note the general condition of all the houses in the area, as well as their size, the quality of landscaping, and the degree of architectural conformity present. These and other factors will help the appraiser determine whether the neighborhood is likely to retain its appearance and value or decline in value.

Most of the categories of information required to complete the Neighborhood Data Form are self-explanatory, but some warrant further explanation.

Figure 4.2 Neighborhood Data Form

NEIGHBORHOOD DATA FORM

BOUNDARIES: | ADJACENT TO:

NORTH _____ | _____

SOUTH _____ | _____

EAST _____ | _____

WEST _____ | _____

TOPOGRAPHY: _____ ☐ URBAN ☐ SUBURBAN ☐ RURAL

STAGE OF LIFE CYCLE OF NEIGHBORHOOD:

☐ GROWTH ☐ EQUILIBRIUM ☐ DECLINE ☐ REVITALIZATION

% BUILT UP: ____ GROWTH RATE: ☐ RAPID ☐ SLOW ☐ STEADY

AVERAGE MARKETING TIME: ____ PROPERTY VALUES: ☐ INCREASING ☐ DECREASING ☐ STABLE

SUPPLY/DEMAND: ☐ OVERSUPPLY ☐ UNDERSUPPLY ☐ BALANCED

CHANGE IN PRESENT LAND USE: _____

POPULATION: ☐ INCREASING ☐ DECREASING ☐ STABLE AVERAGE FAMILY SIZE: _____

AVERAGE FAMILY INCOME _____ INCOME LEVEL: ☐ INCREASING ☐ DECREASING

TYPICAL PROPERTIES:	% OF	AGE	PRICE RANGE	% OWNER OCCUPIED	% RENTALS
VACANT LOTS					
SINGLE-FAMILY RESIDENCES					
2-6-UNIT APARTMENTS					
OVER 6-UNIT APARTMENTS					
NONRESIDENTIAL PROPERTIES					

TAX RATE: _____ ☐ HIGHER ☐ LOWER ☐ SAME AS COMPETING AREAS

SPECIAL ASSESSMENTS OUTSTANDING: _____ EXPECTED: _____

SERVICES: ☐ POLICE ☐ FIRE ☐ GARBAGE COLLECTION OTHER: _____

DISTANCE AND DIRECTION FROM

BUSINESS AREA: _____

COMMERCIAL AREA: _____

PUBLIC ELEMENTARY AND HIGH SCHOOLS: _____

PRIVATE ELEMENTARY AND HIGH SCHOOLS: _____

RECREATIONAL AND CULTURAL AREAS: _____

EXPRESSWAY INTERCHANGE: _____

PUBLIC TRANSPORTATION: _____

TIME TO REACH BUSINESS AREA: _____ COMMERCIAL AREA: _____

EMERGENCY MEDICAL SERVICE: _____

GENERAL TRAFFIC CONDITIONS: _____

PROXIMITY TO HAZARDS (AIRPORT, CHEMICAL STORAGE, ETC.):_____

PROXIMITY TO NUISANCES (SMOKE, NOISE, ETC):_____

Neighborhood Boundaries

In some newer subdivisions, neighborhood boundaries are conspicuously established by a gated entry and walled perimeter. Other neighborhoods, particularly those in older cities, are set off by other factors, such as the following:

- Natural boundaries (actual physical barriers—ravines, lakes, rivers, and highways or other major traffic arteries)
- Differences in land use (changes in zoning from residential to commercial or parkland)
- Average value or age of homes

When filling out the Neighborhood Data Form, the appraiser records the street name or other identifiable dividing line and notes the type of property adjacent to the subject neighborhood at that boundary. A residential property adjacent to a park will usually have a higher value than a similar property adjacent to a commercial property, for instance.

Stage of Life Cycle

A typical neighborhood usually goes through three distinct periods in its life: growth, equilibrium, and decline, which may be followed by revitalization.

Residential property values tend to increase during the period in which an area is first developed. When few vacant building sites remain, the houses in the neighborhood generally reach equilibrium at their highest monetary value, and prices will rarely fluctuate downward. As the years go by, however, and the effects of property deterioration become visible, the area will usually decline both in desirability and value. The process of decline can be accelerated by many factors, including the following:

- Availability of new housing nearby
- Successive ownership of homes by lower-income residents who may not be able to afford the increasing maintenance costs of older homes
- Conversion of some properties to rental units, which may not be properly maintained

As properties decrease in value, some may even be put to a different use, such as light industry, which can further decrease the attractiveness of the surrounding neighborhood for residential use. The life cycle is not always downward, however. It may begin an upswing because of **revitalization** if demand increases and provides the economic stimulus needed for neighborhood renovation. This process has occurred in many cities where the high demand for housing and the desire to avoid a long commute has prompted buyer interest in older homes that offer convenience of location as well as, in some cases, architectural distinctiveness. The **gentrification** of an urban neighborhood can be both a blessing to property owners and a curse to other residents and businesspeople. Renters and merchants may find themselves priced out of their once inexpensive lodgings and establishments as increasing property values prompt higher rental rates.

In general, the classic life-cycle pattern previously described is the result of an overall economic growth coupled with an increasing consumer demand and the availability of land for housing and commercial development. In recent years, this pattern has been subjected to volatile market conditions.

During the 1970s, high interest rates and a prolonged period of economic recession combined with limited land availability to make property ownership increasingly expensive. As a result, the dream of home ownership was placed beyond the means of many more people than it formerly was. Existing housing became much more desirable and, for many, making repairs and improvements to an older building became a viable alternative to buying a new home. In response to this slowing of residential life cycles and the demand for tax-sheltered investments, developers concentrated on commercial structures, such as office buildings, overbuilding many desirable urban and suburban areas.

The 1980s brought a much lower rate of inflation, declining interest rates, and indicators of a general economic recovery that helped revive the sluggish real estate housing market. The number of new building starts rose as demand increased, and the pace of development helped compensate for the slower preceding years. The Tax Reform Act of 1986 greatly limited the use of real estate as a tax shelter, but that limitation emphasized the necessity for prudent investment. A competent appraisal is one of the ways in which the soundness of an investment can be determined.

The country entered the 1990s in a period of overall recession, yet housing costs still represented a significantly greater proportion of living expenses than was true even a decade earlier. The availability of low-interest mortgage loans and loosened credit standards prompted the housing boom that continued into the first part of this century. The subprime mortgage crisis that followed was discussed in Chapter 2.

Demand is not the only influence on property values, however. Social and political decisions by voters and government officials may accelerate or delay the factors that lead to a decline in sales prices. As the population grows (and ages), additional demand for housing of all types is not being automatically met by new development. Financing for new construction has become much more of a hurdle for builders of both small and large developments. In some areas, housing growth is now deliberately limited for environmental or other reasons. When development to meet housing needs is limited, the state of equilibrium of existing housing may be much longer than would otherwise be the case. In other words, homeowners are more likely to repair or remodel their present housing when they can't afford to buy new housing elsewhere, or it simply is unavailable.

Knowledge of the existence of all of these factors and how they are interrelated is part of the appraiser's job. In short, the appraiser must be sensitive to all determinants of value, including economic, social, and governmental influences, to accurately gauge these influences on neighborhood development.

Proximity to Hazards and Nuisances

We are becoming increasingly aware of the importance of the proximity of the neighborhood, or any part of it, to hazards or nuisances. The more we learn about environmental conditions, the more likely we are to discover factors that are injurious to health or safety. The mere potential for danger (such as chemical storage facilities) may lower property values in nearby areas. Active contamination may present an insurmountable barrier to marketability. One of the worst examples in recent years has been the attempted rehabilitation of the Love Canal area of New York. Even after significant remediation efforts, it is questionable whether the majority of the homes that were vacated will ever be reoccupied.

The appraiser should be aware of any existing or potential hazards, as well as ones that have been alleviated.

Site Data Form

The Site Data Form, shown in Figure 4.3, can be used to record the information needed to describe the subject site.

The appraiser begins by obtaining a complete and legally accurate description of the property's location and making a sketch to show the property's approximate shape and street location. A public building or other landmark could also be shown on the sketch to help locate the site. The topography (surface features) of the site should be indicated, along with any natural hazards such as a floodplain, earthquake fault zone, or other potentially dangerous condition.

Other important features of the site are its size in square feet, location in terms of position on the block, utilities, improvements, soil composition, and view. The historically higher value of a corner lot location may not hold true in residential areas with lots 50 feet or more in width and where exposure to busy streets would

Figure 4.3 Site Data Form

SITE DATA FORM

ADDRESS: _____

LEGAL DESCRIPTION: _____

_____

_____

_____

_____

_____

DIMENSIONS: _____

SHAPE: _____ SQUARE FEET: _____

TOPOGRAPHY: _____ VIEW: _____

NATURAL HAZARDS: _____

☐ INSIDE LOT   ☐ CORNER LOT   ☐ FRONTAGE _____

ZONING: _____ ADJACENT AREAS: _____

UTILITIES: ☐ ELECTRICITY   ☐ GAS   ☐ WATER   ☐ TELEPHONE

☐ SANITARY SEWER   ☐ STROM SEWER

IMPROVEMENTS: DRIVEWAY: _____   STREET: _____

SIDEWALK: _____   CURB/GUTTER: _____   ALLEY: _____

STREETLIGHTS: _____

LANDSCAPING: _____

TOPSOIL: _____   DRAINAGE: _____

EASEMENTS: _____

DEED RESTRICTION: _____

SITE PLAT:

be undesirable. The opposite would be true for a commercial site, however, where a high traffic count would be desirable.

Soil composition is always important. If the soil is unable to support a building, piles will have to be driven to carry the weight. On the other hand, bedrock within a few feet of the surface may require blasting before a suitable foundation can be established. In either case, the cost of extraordinary preconstruction site preparation would decrease the site's value.

Knowledge of the subject site's zoning, which will affect its future use, is necessary, as is knowledge of the current zoning of the surrounding areas. A site zoned for a single-family residence may be poorly used for that purpose if multiunit buildings are being built nearby. In such a case, the feasibility of changing the zoning to multiunit residential construction might be analyzed by making a highest and best use study.

Finally, any easements or deed restrictions should be noted. Any part of the site that cannot be used for building purposes should be clearly designated, along with any other limitations on site use. Such limitations could raise or lower site value. An easement, for example, may allow airspace or below-ground space for present or future utility installations. Another kind of easement may give an adjoining property owner the right to travel over the property. Deed restrictions, usually set up by the property's subdivider, may specify the size of lots used for building, the type or style of building constructed, setbacks from property lines, or other factors designed to increase the subdivision's homogeneity and thus stabilize property values.

Building Data Form

The Building Data Form, shown in Figure 4.4, can be used to appraise a single-family residence. Not all categories of information will apply to every house, however. The appraiser can draw a line through any item that does not apply to a particular property.

Even before entering a single-family house, the appraiser is called on to make certain judgments. Approaching the house from the street, the appraiser makes a note of the first impression created by the house, its orientation, and how it fits in with the surrounding area. At the same time, the appraiser notes and records information about the landscaping. Next, the external construction materials (for the foundation, outside walls, roof, driveway, etc.) and the condition of each are listed, and the general external condition of the building is rated. Finally, the appraiser measures each structure on the site, sketches its dimensions, and computes its area in square feet.

Figure 4.4 Building Data Form

BUILDING DATA FORM

ADDRESS: _____

NO. OF UNITS: _____ NO. OF STORIES: _____ ORIENTATION: N S E W

TYPE: _____ DESIGN: _____ AGE: _____ SQUARE FEET: _____

	GOOD	FAIR	POOR
GENERAL CONDITION OF EXTERIOR			
FOUNDATION TYPE _____ BSMT./CRAWL SP./SLAB			
EXTERIOR WALLS: BRICK/BLOCK/VENEER/STUCCO/			
WOOD/COMPOSITE/ALUMINUM/VINYL			
WINDOW FRAMES: METAL/WOOD			
STORM WINDOWS: _____ SCREENS: ____			
GARAGE: _____ ATTACHED/DETACHED			
NUMBER OF CARS: _____			
☐ PORCH ☐ DECK ☐ PATIO ☐ SHED			
OTHER: _____			
GENERAL CONDITION OF INTERIOR			
INTERIOR WALLS: DRY WALL/PLASTER/WOOD			
CEILINGS: _____			
FLOORS: WOOD/CONCRETE/TILE/CARPET			
ELECTRICAL WIRING AND SERVICE: _____			
HEATING PLANT: _____ AGE: _____			
GAS/OIL/WOOD/ELECTRIC/SOLAR			
CENTRAL AIR-CONDITIONING: _____ AIR FILTRATION: ___			
NO OF FIREPLACES: _____ TYPE: _____			
OTHER _____			
BATHROOM: FLOOR___WALLS_____FIXTURES _____			
BATHROOM: FLOOR___WALLS_____FIXTURES _____			
BATHROOM: FLOOR___WALLS_____FIXTURES _____			
KITCHEN: FLOOR___WALLS_____CABINETS _____			
FIXTURES _____			

ROOM SIZES	LIVING ROOM	DINING ROOM	KITCHEN	BEDROOM	BATH	CLOSETS	FAMILY ROOM
BASEMENT							
1ST FLOOR							
2ND FLOOR							
ATTIC							

DEPRECIATION (DESCRIBE):

PHYSICAL DETERIORATION _____

FUNCTIONAL OBSOLESCENCE _____

EXTERNAL OBSOLESCENCE_____

Inside the house, the appraiser notes and evaluates major construction details and fixtures, particularly the following:

- Interior finish
- Kind of floors, walls, and doors
- Condition and adequacy of kitchen cabinets
- Type and condition of heating and air-conditioning systems
- Rooms with special features, such as built-in bookcases and fireplaces
- All other features that indicate the quality of construction

The appraiser also observes the general condition of the house for evidence of recent remodeling, cracked plaster, sagging floors, or any other signs of deterioration, and records room dimensions and total square footage.

The appraiser then notes the general condition of the building, giving consideration to three kinds of depreciation:

1. *Physical deterioration.* This is the effect of ordinary wear and tear and the action of the elements.

2. *Functional obsolescence.* This results from the inadequacy of features in the design, layout, or construction of the building that are currently desired by purchasers, or the presence of features that have become unfashionable or unnecessary. Fixtures such as bathtubs or vanities also fall into this category. A kitchen without updated cabinets, countertops, and appliances would be undesirable in most areas.

3. *External obsolescence.* This is the result of physical or economic conditions outside the property. A change of zoning from residential to commercial might make a single-family house obsolete if such usage does not fully utilize (take full monetary advantage of) the site.

The kinds of depreciation and how each affects the value of the property are explained in greater detail in the chapters on the specific appraisal approaches. When the appraiser first records the building data, it is enough to make a general estimate of the degree of physical deterioration, functional obsolescence, or external obsolescence present in the property.

An appraiser cannot determine some property features without actually taking the building apart. If all of the items on the Building Data Form have been noted and recorded, however, the appraiser should be able to identify most of the building's deficiencies, as well as its special features. Information received only from the owner or from some other source and which is not personally verified by the appraiser can be recorded, but the source of the information should be supplied. For instance, the owner may know, or may have been told, that the house has wall, floor, and ceiling insulation rated R-19 (a measure of insulation performance, explained further in the next chapter). If so, that information and its source should be noted.

As you read through the rest of this book, you will be filling out the forms presented in this chapter. Keep in mind that no standardized form can ever be perfectly suited to every type of property. Also, significant regional differences exist across the United States, in both building design and construction. Climatic requirements probably account for the greatest number of construction variables. The basement that is highly desirable in the Midwest or Northeast as a cold barrier, storage area, and (increasingly) home office or entertainment space may be an expensive oddity in the West or Southwest. Design is very often dictated by local tastes, influenced over the years by the availability of construction materials. The ground-hugging adobe house typical of the Santa Fe style would look out of place among the wood-sided homes of a New England village.

As you complete the Appraisal Worksheet that follows, be sure to record any distinct regional property characteristics that contribute to value. In addition, note any unusual property characteristics that may detract from value.

APPRAISAL WORKSHEET

1. What are the boundaries of the immediate neighborhood?_____
    _____

2. Categorize the neighborhood as urban, suburban, or rural._____
    _____

3. In what stage of the life cycle (growth, equilibrium, decline, or revitalization) is the neighborhood?_____

4   What is the average family income in the neighborhood?_____

5. What percentage of properties are rental units?_____

6. What percentage of properties in the neighborhood are single-family residences?_____ Two- to six-unit apartment buildings? _____ Larger apartment buildings?_____ Vacant lots?_____ Nonresidential buildings?_____

7. What is the property tax rate?_____ How does it compare to the rate in nearby areas? _____

8. What special assessments must property owners pay, and how do these compare to assessments in other areas? _____
    _____

APPRAISAL WORKSHEET (continued)

9. How far is the house from the business area, schools, and other amenities?_____
    _____

10. Are there any hazards or nuisances in the neighborhood or nearby?_____ If so,
    identify them and their proximity to the house. _____

11. What is the legal description of the property?_____
    _____

12. What is the size, shape, and topography of the lot?_____
    _____

13. What is the property's zoning classification?_____
    _____

14. Are there any easements across the property and, if so, what are they?_____
    _____

15. List any restrictions in the deed to the property._____
    _____
    _____

16. Describe the design and general outside features of the house and the house's
    overall condition. _____
    _____
    _____

17. Describe the interior features of the house, including floor and wall coverings and
    kitchen cabinetry and countertops, and note their condition._____
    _____
    _____
    _____

18. What kind of electrical service does the house have?_____

19. Describe the home's heating plant and air-conditioning or cooling system, if any.
    _____
    _____

20. Note the number and size of the rooms in the house, as well as its total square
    footage._____
    _____
    _____

The Neighborhood and the Home

5

When an appraiser compares properties to determine value, it is critical that the properties come from the same neighborhood or very similar neighborhoods. The attributes of the surrounding area are just as important as the size, quality of construction, and features of the home being appraised. In order to be sure that a property is similar to another property in both on-site and off-site characteristics, the appraiser must provide a thorough description of the subject property and its surroundings.

Location, Location, Location

Most people who have shopped for a home have heard the old maxim that the three most important factors that contribute to property value are location, location, and location. A house in a desirable location—a place where people want to live and work—is always in demand and is usually in limited supply. In general, property values tend to increase at a pace at least equal to the inflation rate, but most homes—especially well-located, single-family homes—appreciate at a much higher rate. Location has a direct effect on the market value of property and will greatly influence a person's enjoyment of the house.

A **neighborhood** is typically defined by subdivision boundaries, geographic features (such as a canyon), or man-made features (such as roadways). An appraiser will try to find recently sold properties in the same neighborhood as the property being appraised, which are located as close as possible to the subject property. Distances between properties are usually a good indicator of their validity for appraisal purposes. If building lots are less than a quarter-acre, there should be plenty of comparable properties within a one-mile (or less) radius. If the area has six-acre minimum zoning, the search for recently sold similar properties may need to be expanded to several miles. The objective is to find sales that represent the appraised property as closely as possible in all respects.

Neighborhood Development

As we already noted in chapter 4, neighborhoods generally go through several stages as they are developed. When an area is first developed and experiences growth of population and businesses, property values usually increase until few vacant sites remain. At that point, property values in the neighborhood tend to stabilize at their highest monetary value relative to other properties in the area, and prices rarely fluctuate downward.

A period of decline begins when a neighborhood can no longer compete with comparable neighborhoods, or when new development makes newer homes with more desirable amenities available. During this period, prices may fail to attract buyers and "For Sale" signs may appear more frequently.

When a community has been completely developed, a neighborhood's life cycle may start over again due to revitalization—a period when the unavailability of newer or more affordable alternatives means that demand for existing homes increases, providing the stimulus needed for neighborhood renovation.

It is the appraiser's job to build an accurate profile of the neighborhood. The appraiser knows which areas are seeing declining interest and which neighborhoods are "hot." Once compiled and analyzed, this information will be changed as often as warranted. New neighborhood data will not have to be compiled for each appraisal, because many of the appraisals to be made will be within the same neighborhood. Some categories of neighborhood data will have to be updated at least annually, and significant change in any recorded data should be noted.

Evaluating the Neighborhood

Comparing neighborhoods is probably the most important step an appraiser can take before valuing a house in a new community. A buyer wants to be sure that the neighborhood offers the right living environment for a family's lifestyle. At the same time, it is just as important to view the home as an investment whose future value will be greatly influenced by the neighborhood's evolution, whether the location is in a long-established city or one that is still being developed.

A neighborhood not only affects the market value of a home, it shapes the way people live. Where will children go to school? How long will it take residents to get to work? Does the area have a low crime rate, or does every home have burglar bars on the windows? The neighborhood affects dozens of other everyday matters.

It may ultimately make more difference to a family than the home itself. From the appraiser's perspective, the neighborhood of the property being appraised is defined so that the appraiser can find recent property sales in the same neighborhood or one like it.

The location of the home within the neighborhood can't be ignored. Is a big-box retail store being planned for the usually quiet city shopping street behind the home, which will greatly increase the movement of trucks and customer vehicles in the area—and make on-street parking a hassle for residents? The quiet enjoyment of a dream house near the entrance to a brand-new subdivision could turn into a nightmare for the homeowner if a lumberyard opens across the road or a 24-hour gas station/convenience store is built on the corner.

The appraiser also will want to make sure that the home being valued is in the same general price range as surrounding homes. There may be no other homes comparable to the biggest, most expensive home on the block, which will not have the same resale value in a moderately priced neighborhood as it would if it were located in a neighborhood of comparably or higher-priced homes. As a general rule, appraisers and mortgage lenders have found that the resale value of a relatively inexpensive home in a good area will be pulled up by the higher-priced homes, while the large, expensive home will be pulled down by surrounding lower-priced homes.

Corner lots in some subdivisions are sometimes preferred because they may be larger than other lots, but they will have more traffic noise. An inside lot may offer more privacy, particularly if most lots are fenced. In a subdivision with curvilinear streets, there may not be any homes on a traditional corner lot, but other factors may come into play to make some properties more or less desirable than others, such as a location at the top of a t-shaped intersection, facing oncoming traffic.

How Far Is the Outside World?

When describing a neighborhood, the appraiser checks the distance to the nearest police station and fire department. Property owners will also want easy access to shopping, schools, places of worship, libraries, recreation areas, medical facilities, banks, the post office, and public transportation.

A quick drive around the area will give a fair picture of what is and is not within walking distance of homes in the area. A satellite image from Google Earth and other Internet sites can find the neighborhood, pinpoint the exact locations of schools, public offices, restaurants, grocery stores, and other services, and even show the constellations visible in the night sky. The Google Earth software can be downloaded free from *www.googleearth.com*.

Quality of Schools

If a homeowner has children, the quality of schools will be an important consideration. A few visits and phone calls can help separate rumors and opinions from facts. The local school district can provide statistics on class size, achievement test scores, and dollars spent per student, but a school visit will also be revealing. A great deal of information may be available from the district's website. There are also web services, such as *www.greatschools.net* or *www.schoolmatters. com* that provide publicly available information, ratings, and parent and student comments.

Homeowners without children may be satisfied with a community where education is not a big-budget item, but they will also want to keep future salability of the property in mind. Homeowners in some senior citizen communities, such as Sun City, Arizona, don't pay school taxes.

The Importance of Essential Services

A utility company can truthfully claim that the best compliment is to be taken for granted. It's easy to take running water, reliable electricity and natural gas service, police and fire protection, sewer systems, garbage collection, maintained roadways, and snow removal for granted, especially if you are presently living in an area where these services are provided.

The appraiser doesn't take anything for granted. The appraiser will check into the availability and quality of all services. For example, is there a municipal water supply? What is its source? The Environmental Protection Agency (EPA) requires information on the levels of contaminants in the water supply to be made available to consumers.

In some suburbs or in a rural area, the house may have a well. How deep is it? Has it ever been known to go dry? How old is the pump? Well water may have a strong iron or sulfur taste, or it may taste great, depending on its location. Is there an adequate water purification system? If the area is noted for the hardness (mineral content) of its water, is there a water softener to remove minerals and extend the life of the home's plumbing system? The property may have access to a municipal water supply for household use and well water for irrigation—a cost-effective combination.

If the community has storm sewers, are they adequate for the area? Have there been any problems with sewers backing up in basements? Have heavy rains caused repeated flooding or severe runoff conditions that might present a health hazard or impair the foundation of the house?

Is fire protection provided by a full-time or voluntary department? While volunteers have demonstrated exceptional skill in fighting fires, a paid fire department is usually better equipped and more responsive to alarms. Insurance companies usually set lower rates for fire insurance in areas that have paid fire departments, and an individual property may have a lower insurance rate if a fire hydrant is located on or near it.

Limitations on Property Use

Most local governments use ordinances to specify the minimum size house that can be constructed on a particular lot. They also specify how close you can build to the street and adjacent property lines. By regulating what can and cannot be built, communities protect residential neighborhoods from unwanted or poorly located commercial developments. Thoughtfully zoned areas that provide essential services in a layout planned for easy access tend to hold their property values. This will be important for homeowners when it comes time to sell.

The zoning classification of nearby undeveloped land is important, too. Today's empty field could be tomorrow's school, shopping center, or stadium. The cautious person moving to a new city who wisely buys a house on a quiet street in a beautiful neighborhood will be dismayed when plans are announced for a highway extension that will go through the meadow behind the house.

As mentioned in the first chapter of this book, deeds to properties in many subdivisions carry private restrictions that regulate the size of the house and the materials used to build it. Some even restrict architectural styles and color selections. Individual deeds typically reference a master deed containing the property restrictions that can be found in the public records. Property can also be subject to the rules of a homeowners' association. A prospective homebuyer should be given a copy of all applicable deed restrictions and homeowners' association rules. As a general rule, the appraiser will look for properties that have the same restrictions as the property being appraised.

Environmental Concerns

During all this legwork in the neighborhood, the appraiser should stop and take a deep breath—literally. Is the air clean? Are there noxious odors that may indicate the presence of an undesirable manufacturing facility? Does the topography of the area create a natural collection point for pollution? Smog problems are worse in some areas than others, even in the same city. A picturesque valley may become a smoke-filled health hazard during seasons when fireplaces are in use. Some communities restrict wood burning for a variety of physical and environmental safety reasons.

Environmental conditions such as smoke, noxious fumes, and brownfields (toxic waste dumps and old landfills) may not only threaten the health of neighborhood residents, they can have a significant negative effect on the value and marketability of property in the area. The appraiser should know enough about the area to identify potential problems—and also note when those problems have been alleviated. Ironically, as industrial production has moved from cities to rural areas (and increasingly to other countries), some urban areas that would have been unthinkable for residential development a generation ago are now sought after for loft conversions, townhouses, and other residential and commercial development. Once cleaned up, such areas can be desirable because of their proximity to the business district; in addition, they often offer locations on (or views of) waterways that were once industrial highways but have now been restored to a condition that showcases their natural beauty.

The appraiser listens, too. How noisy is the area? Can you hear the distant drone of cars on a freeway or trucks grinding around an interchange? Is there a factory or airport nearby? Noise doesn't even have to be nearby to be irritating. If there are no intervening obstructions, sound can carry for miles.

Traffic Patterns

A large volume of traffic going through a neighborhood on a residential street (through traffic) may present a safety hazard and create noise and pollution. If a family has small children, a constant stream of traffic should cause some anxiety. Although neighborhoods in communities built before 1950 typically have streets laid out in a traditional grid pattern—that is, streets at right angles—newer neighborhoods make use of curving and dead-end (no outlet) streets to help slow the speed of traffic and reduce its volume. Families who want increased safety for their children (and quieter living) will look for cul-de-sacs and looping streets off main roads.

Sidewalks can increase safety for pedestrians of any age. In addition, a dedicated walking/bicycle path is a desirable amenity that can keep walkers and bicyclists away from traffic, help buffer homes from roadways, and provide attractive landscaping around a community.

The checklist in Figure 5.1 can be used to analyze and evaluate the neighborhood in which the subject property is located. After checking out all these points carefully, the appraiser will be ready to focus on the attributes of the specific site.

Figure 5.1 How Does the Neighborhood Rate?

	YES	NO
1. Surrounding houses conform architecturally?	___	___
2. Homes in the area in the same general price range?	___	___
3. Homes well cared for?	___	___
4. Landscaping well kept?	___	___
5. Adequate police and fire protection?	___	___
6. All utilities available?	___	___
7. Shopping, schools, parks, medical facilities, and recreation areas nearby?	___	___
8. Convenient to place of employment?	___	___
9. Owner occupied?	___	___
10. Trash collection, snow removal, and road maintenance available?	___	___
11. Who lives there—ages, income, children, interests?_____		
12. Access to public transportation?	___	___
13. Taxes in line with competing areas?	___	___
14. Special assessments?	___	___
15. Property values rising?	___	___
16. Good schools?	___	___
17. Current or anticipated zoning restrictions?	___	___
18. Radon contamination in the area?	___	___
19. Good quality of water?	___	___
20. Hazardous traffic patterns?	___	___
21. Irritating noise levels from cars, trucks, airplanes, trains, or buses?	___	___
22. Adequate parking?	___	___
23. Leash laws for pets?	___	___
24. Street paving in good condition?	___	___
25. Plans for expansion and development?	___	___

Residential Construction and Home Inspection

6

To appraise a home, you first must check its neighborhood for livability and investment potential. Next, you must analyze and evaluate its site. Finally, you must inspect the house itself and give an opinion about its condition. An appraiser must methodically check the house's interior design, the physical condition of its foundation, structural framework, interior and exterior surfaces, and mechanical systems. Obviously, a basic understanding of construction is an extremely handy aptitude to possess. An appraiser must look beyond the visible charm and appeal of the house and view it with a cold, objective attitude and with the trained eye of a detective. A person conducting an appraisal must also be able to ask questions and to find answers.

This chapter considers various factors of the neighborhood, lot, and house that contribute to and detract from value and resale potential. It also covers the basics of new home construction.

SITE

After the appraiser has considered the neighborhood, he or she will focus on the site.

Orientation: Locating the House on the Site

The site should be an integral part of the design of a house. Correct siting on the property can make the house more pleasant to live in and more attractive to buyers when it is placed on the market. The site should be analyzed for its topography, the variations in the sun's path from season to season, the types and sizes of trees, the views, the noise, and the proximity to neighbors. Once these factors are studied, the builder can properly orient the house to take full advantage of the site's special characteristics. For example, if the land is built up, the house should be located on the highest point so that rainwater drains away from the house.

When orienting a house for maximum natural light, builders should be aware that morning sun is from the east and evening sun from the west. Midday sun is from the south, and in winter the sun is far to the south, making it an excellent heat source. The north side of the house receives no direct sunlight and may be a good location for bedrooms.

With good site planning, outdoor space is designed for three different functions: public use, service use, and private use. The public space or zone is the area visible from the street—usually the land in front of the house—and concern should be taken about the impression it makes on people driving by or coming to the main entrance. Zoning regulations specify how far back a house must be placed on a lot. The service zone consists of the driveway, the walks, and the areas where trash and garbage can be collected and outdoor equipment can be stored. It should be designed so that deliveries can be made to the service entrance without intrusion into space intended only for private use. The private zone is the outdoor living space for the family. It may include a patio, a deck and hot tub, a built-in barbecue, fire pit, a garden, and a play area for children.

In most cases, a minimum amount of valuable land should be allocated for public and service use and the maximum amount for private enjoyment. Thus, architects prefer to situate a house near the street to provide a larger backyard.

Use the checklist in Figure 6.1 for an examination of the subject site.

Figure 6.1 Site Checklist

	YES	NO
1. Does the site have all the necessary utilities?	___	___
2. Is the site well landscaped?	___	___
3. Does the landscaping provide privacy?	___	___
4. Does the topography of the land allow for good drainage?	___	___
5. Are the public, service, and private zones of the site well defined?	___	___
6. Have you checked on any easements or deed restrictions?	___	___
7. Is the size of the site standard within the neighborhood?	___	___
8. Does the house take good advantage of natural conditions (sun, breeze, view)?	___	___

Next is the house itself. Because most houses today are constructed with wood frames, this chapter will focus on the elements involved in the construction and design of wood-frame residences.

BUILDING CODES

The purpose of building codes is to ensure that builders follow minimum standards for construction. Different codes may be in effect in specific regions of the country. These include the Uniform Building Code, the National Electric Code, and the Uniform Plumbing Code, plus any state and local codes. Some cities, for example, have new energy codes that require an entire house to conform to code if new rooms are added. In such a case, the builder may be required to install new windows throughout the house even if the homeowner is adding only a bedroom. The local building department can provide information on any such requirements.

PLANS AND SPECIFICATIONS

Detailed plans and specifications are required to comply with building codes. Working drawings, called plans or blueprints, show the construction details of the house, while specifications are written instructions that tell the builder what materials to use, where to use them, and what results to expect.

ARCHITECTURAL STYLES

Although construction details are rigidly specified by building codes, house styles may vary greatly. No absolute standards exist, and real estate values rest on what potential buyers, users, and investors think is desirable, as well as on what they consider to be attractive.

The outward appearance of a home may adhere to one style only or a combination of several different styles. A house shouldn't be a mishmash of details, however—a little something for everybody. Materials, scale, and proportion must be consistent with the architectural style. For example, if windows are not properly placed and sized, there's always going to be something not quite right about the home's appearance. Colonial brick on a Spanish ranch is a waste of two good ideas. Over the years, a home that's true to its design will mature gracefully and always be in good taste. Figure 6.2 shows several house styles that have been popular for many years.

The architectural style of a home provides long-range appeal to users and investors. The factors that affect appeal are difficult to identify and differ according to style trends and individual preferences and tastes.

Figure 6.2 House Styles

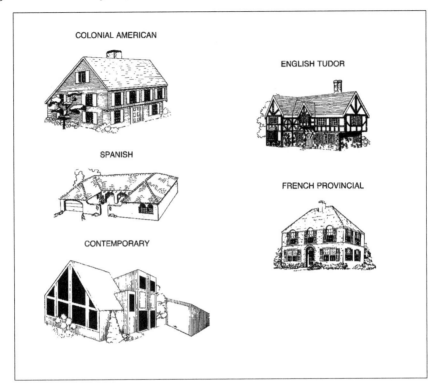

HOUSE TYPES

House type refers to the number of and arrangement of a home's living levels. Although variations exist, most home types fall somewhere within the basic categories described next and illustrated in Figure 6.3.

Ranch

The ranch is a one-story, low-to-the-ground structure with all of the habitable rooms on one level. The classic ranch style features deep roof overhangs for protection from the elements.

Raised Ranch

This is a ranch house with the basement area raised slightly out of the ground and which has two distinct levels and no entry between levels. Stairs from the outside usually lead up to the main-level living area.

Split-Level

This generic term applies to any house that has floors located halfway between other floors.

Split-Entry

This is a modified split-level. The entry is on grade (ground level) or just a few steps above grade, with the main level half a flight down from the entry. Typically, part of the lower level is above ground to admit natural light into the space and make the lower level more livable.

Figure 6.3 House Types

Figure 6.3 (*Continued*)

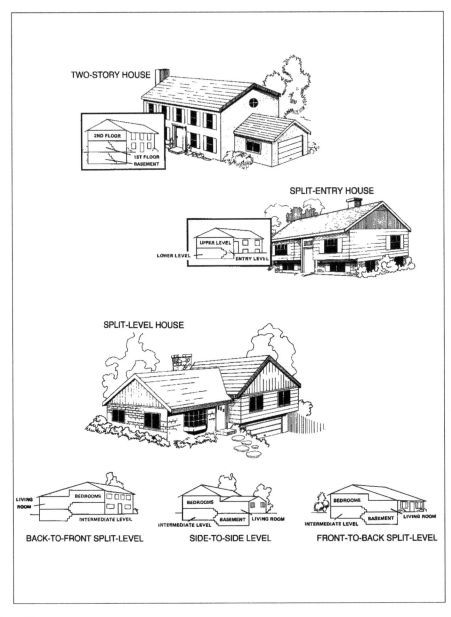

Two-Story

This is a house with two complete stories above ground, connected by a full flight of stairs. The two-story house offers the greatest amount of living space within an established perimeter. Because the living area is doubled on the same foundation, it also has a lower price per square foot than a single-story house.

Story-and-a-Half

Often called a Cape Cod, this house has a full flight of stairs connecting two levels. The roofline usually starts at or just a few feet above the floor of the second story and peaks to allow headroom in about half of the second-story space.

INTERIOR DESIGN

The interior design or layout of a house is central not only to day-to-day comfort and livability, but it affects the home's market value as well.

Two basic approaches to space must be taken into account when designing a floor plan—open and casual or separate and formal. In an open plan, fewer walls and use of half-walls create an airy atmosphere that makes spaces seem larger. Activities can overlap from room to room. On the negative side, energy costs are usually increased, and often some privacy is lost. Fewer interior walls can also mean limited spots for furniture placement.

In a less open plan, areas can be closed off to control sound or to direct heating and cooling. If more private areas are desired, natural light should be provided by windows and skylights to avoid a closed-in look. Spaces should flow well and not appear chopped up.

Floor Plan

Living with a floor plan that doesn't feel right or doesn't conform to a family's lifestyle is like wearing a shoe that doesn't fit. The family will never get used to it, and they will always wish they had something else. So before deciding on a floor plan, a prospective buyer should take a good look at the layout and imagine how it will feel living in the spaces.

A good floor plan directs traffic smoothly and usually divides neatly into three basic areas or zones: working, or high-activity areas; living, or moderate-activity areas; and sleeping, or low-activity areas. The working zone includes the kitchen, laundry area, and perhaps a workshop. The living zone consists of the living, dining, and family rooms. The sleeping zone contains the bedrooms. Each zone should be separated from the others so that activities in one area do not interfere with those in another. Ideally, the areas that generate the most noise should be grouped together, well away from the bedrooms.

Circulation Areas

Circulation areas, consisting of halls, stairways, and entries, often make the difference between a good floor plan and a poor one.

The main entry to the house should be easily accessible to visitors. Guests should have only a short walk from the sidewalk or driveway to the front door. Also, the view from the entry that will greet visitors must be considered. Can the kitchen be seen when visitors come through the door? A refrigerator, for instance, shouldn't be the first thing to catch the eye. Entries, remember, are where first impressions take shape.

Another important consideration in any plan is the garage-to-kitchen connection. Is there a short and convenient route for unloading groceries or taking out garbage?

A study of a floor plan will reveal traffic patterns. Can people get directly from one room to another without crossing other rooms? Is there direct access to a bathroom from any room? Is the stairway between levels located off a hallway or foyer rather than off a room?

Other Principles of Good Design

A kitchen contains three main activity areas or centers:

1. *Food storage.* This includes the refrigerator/freezer, cabinets, and counter space.
2. *Cooking.* This includes the range, oven, counter space on either side, and cabinets and drawers for pots, pans, and utensils.
3. *Cleanup.* This includes the sink, counter space on either side, a garbage disposal, a dishwasher, and a trash compactor.

The efficient arrangement of these three centers is called a work triangle (see Figure 6.4). The dimensions of the triangle will depend on the size of the room, but the work area should be unobstructed.

Figure 6.4   Kitchen Work Triangle

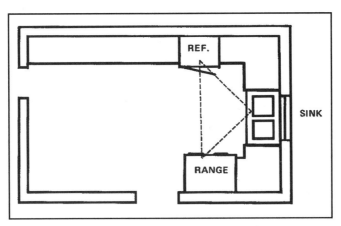

To save steps and time, short, direct routes should connect the kitchen with all eating areas. If traffic goes through the kitchen, it should pass outside the work triangle so people won't bump into each other when someone is working at the stove.

For cooks who like to keep in touch with the family or guests while preparing meals, a kitchen that's open to the family room is ideal. This arrangement makes the space seem larger and provides a place for countertop meals.

If a family enjoys entertaining, or appreciates dining variety, the floor plan must cater to an assortment of dining options, whether they include an informal eating area, countertop, or formal dining room. All these areas must be contiguous to a food-preparation and serving location. If the family is fond of barbecuing in the backyard, a plan with an outdoor deck or patio adjacent to the kitchen is ideal.

Whatever layout is chosen for the dining and living areas, plenty of space should be available for furnishings and activities. If entertaining in small groups is desired, a family room that's cozier and more specialized than a formal living room would be preferred. A formal living room, however, offers the flexibility of an intimate conversation or reading area.

Privacy is the key to any successful bedroom arrangement. Sleeping areas should be secluded from living and working areas, especially for families with children or for those who entertain frequently.

In the master bath, locating the vanity in a separate area from the toilet, tub, and shower makes it easier for a couple to get ready for the day and will also keep the mirror from steaming up from the hot water in the tub and shower. If a person enjoys relaxing after a stressful day by taking a hot bath, lifting weights, or doing aerobics, the possibility of including a convenient exercise area, sauna, or whirlpool tub should be considered.

A full bath near the secondary bedrooms adds to the convenience and privacy of other family members and overnight guests. A half-bath near the kitchen and living areas will keep guests from invading the home's private spaces.

Laundry facilities should be placed close to bedrooms and bathrooms. Proximity to the kitchen and an outside entrance combines laundry and mud room functions. A two-laundry setup is common in large homes.

Figure 6.5 lists the main flaws to watch for when evaluating a floor plan.

Throughout the rest of this chapter, many construction terms and concepts will be presented and discussed. As needed, refer to the Anatomy of a House diagram at the end of this chapter. The diagram identifies the different parts of a house and shows how they fit together as a whole.

Figure 6.5   Floor Plan Checklist

		YES	NO
1.	Are main interior zones—living, working, sleeping—clearly separated?	___	___
2.	Does the front door enter into a foyer—not directly into the living room?	___	___
3.	Is there a front hall closet?	___	___
4.	Is there direct access from the front door to the kitchen, bathroom, and bedrooms without passing through other rooms?	___	___
5.	Is the rear door convenient to the kitchen and easy to reach from the street, driveway, and garage?	___	___
6.	Is there a comfortable eating space for the family in or near the kitchen?	___	___
7.	Is a separate dining area or dining room convenient to the kitchen?	___	___
8.	Is a stairway located in a hallway or foyer instead of between levels of a room?	___	___
9.	Are bedrooms concealed from the living room or foyer?	___	___
10.	Are walls between bedrooms soundproof? (They should be separated by a bathroom or closet.)	___	___
11.	Is the family room well located?	___	___
12.	Is the basement accessible from outside?	___	___
13.	Are outdoor living areas accessible from the kitchen?	___	___
14.	Are there enough doors and windows to provide adequate natural light?	___	___
15.	Does the kitchen have enough storage space? Counter space? Lighting?	___	___
16.	Is the work triangle efficient?	___	___
17.	Are kitchen work areas separate from heavy traffic areas?	___	___
18.	Is the kitchen up to date?	___	___
19.	Does the house have a full bathroom on each floor?	___	___
20.	Is there adequate closet space throughout the house?	___	___
21.	Is the laundry area in a satisfactory location?	___	___
22.	Is the garage wide and long enough?	___	___
23.	Does the garage have close access to the kitchen?	___	___

The Value of Home Improvements

Remodeling can make a house more valuable as well as more livable. Although the cash invested in improvements seldom yields a dollar-for-dollar return when the

Figure 6.6 Remodeling Projects and How They Pay Off

Type of Improvement (mid-range)	Recovery Cost %
1. Room addition	72%
2. Major kitchen remodeling	80
3. Minor kitchen remodeling	85
4. New bath	75
5. Bathroom remodeling	85
6. Master suite	73
7. Roof replacement	74
8. Finished basement	79
9. Garage	40
10. Window replacement (vinyl)	84
11. Window replacement (wood)	85
12. New heating system	90
13. Deck	77
14. Sunroom addition	66
15. Central air	75
16. Siding replacement	87
17. Exterior painting	65
18. Home office remodel	63
19. Landscaping (minor)	50
20. Energy-efficient fireplace	75
21. Interior painting	73

house is sold, some remodeling projects do promise to return more of the investment than others. Keep in mind, however, that no matter how much is invested in improvements, ultimately, it's the marketplace that determines what the home is worth.

Figure 6.6 shows the payback potential of 21 popular remodeling projects. These percentages vary across the country and year-to-year.

FOUNDATION

A foundation supports the weight of the house and its contents (see Figure 6.7). It is the substructure on which the superstructure rests. The foundation includes the footings, foundation walls, pilasters, slab, and all other parts that provide support for the house and distribute the weight of the superstructure to the underlying earth.

Figure 6.7 Foundation

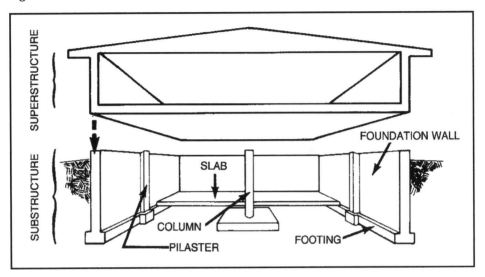

Poured concrete is by far the best of all foundation materials. Because of its strength and resistance to moisture, it is particularly good for keeping basements dry. Other foundations may be constructed of cut stone, stone and brick, and concrete block.

Exterior Foundation Inspection

Walk around the perimeter of the house and inspect the foundation. The foundation should be exposed for six to eight inches aboveground. Pay particular attention to any areas that appear to be settling. Settlement is caused by the compression of soil under the foundation. All houses settle. The uneven settlement of the foundation, especially at the corners, however, is a sure sign of trouble. Uneven settlement is evidenced also by cracks in foundation walls, cracks in finished walls and ceilings, floors that slope, and windows and doors that fit poorly.

Check for cracks and signs of water penetration. Peeling paint on a concrete foundation may indicate moisture buildup in the basement. Soil should be graded away from the foundation to allow runoff water to flow away from the house. Look for signs of runoff pooling against the foundation. Check to see that downspouts have splash plates to channel water away.

Basement

A basement is the lowest level of a house and is usually left unfinished by the builder. The exterior walls of a basement are also the foundation walls of the house. Exposed foundation walls can tell you a lot about the structural soundness of the house. For example, curves or bows in the foundation walls may indicate excessive weight being applied to that area.

Does the basement smell musty or feel damp? Look for signs of water penetration—discoloration along the lower wall surfaces; white powdery deposits, called efflorescence, on exposed concrete (mineral salts in masonry that dissolve in water and pass through to the surface); damp wood sills (these rest on the foundation and support the wall framing); or discoloration of framing members.

Check the location of any foundation cracks identified on your external examination. Does water appear to have entered through them? A leaky basement is one of the biggest headaches a homeowner can have, and it is often difficult and expensive to correct.

Termite Damage and Wood Rot

Before concrete for the foundation is poured, the ground should be chemically treated to poison termites, which are antlike insects that are very destructive to wood. This will prevent them from coming up through or around the foundation and into the wooden structure. The chemical treatment of the lumber used for sills and beams and the installation of metal termite shields will also provide protection.

When checking for termites, look for fuzzy white columns of tubes snaking up the foundation. Termites and wood rot can destroy wood from the inside, with little visible evidence. Examine any wood adjacent to the foundation, such as siding or porch supports. If you question its soundness, probe it with a screwdriver. If the wood feels like cork, it has been eaten away inside.

Carpenter Ants and Powder-Post Beetles

Carpenter ants and powder-post beetles are other insects that cause damage to wood. Damage by carpenter ants can be recognized by the presence of hollow, irregular, clean chambers cut across the grain of partially decayed wood. The most obvious sign of powder-post beetles are small round holes in the infested wood. The beetles exit through these holes after they have done their work.

Radon Gas

Radon is a colorless, odorless, tasteless radioactive gas found in most rocks and soils. Outdoors, it mixes with the air and is found in low concentrations that are harmless to people. Indoors, however, it can accumulate and build up to dangerous levels that can increase the risk of lung cancer.

Besides the most immediate concern about radon—the threat of cancer—homeowners are also worried about the impact of high radon levels on the value of real estate. A seller may be held responsible retroactively for corrective measures if testing shows that a house was sold with known dangerously high levels of radon gas. In some states, sellers must give written notice of any problems affecting the value of the property being sold. In other states, the potential for a dangerous level of radon to be present in a home must be disclosed, even if radon testing has not been conducted. The problem is that radon gas levels may vary from day to day and even week to week. They are affected by barometric pressure, rainfall, wind, and temperature. Remediation can be as simple as a fan that vents basement air to the outside of the home.

Figure 6.8 shows how radon gas can enter a home.

Figure 6.8 Common Radon Entry Routes

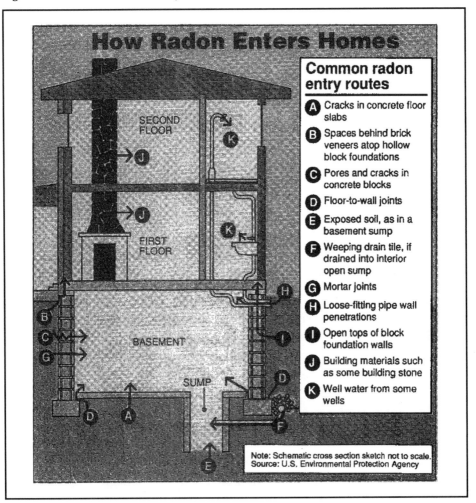

FRAMING

After the foundation is in place, the house is ready for framing. A house's frame, or skeleton, gives shape and strength to the building. It is usually made of pieces of lumber nailed together to create a framework of floors, walls, and roof. The frame is then covered with sheets of insulating material or plywood.

After the skeleton of the house is constructed, sheathing is nailed directly to the wall studs to form the base for siding. Plywood panels used to be the most popular sheathing material for walls and are a good choice in earthquake-prone areas. In other areas, they are sometimes used on corners to lend stability, paired with better insulators such as fiberboard combinations and polyurethane foam panels.

The roof on a house does more to set it apart from other houses than any other single architectural feature. Some of the most commonly used roof styles or designs are shown in Figure 6.9.

EXTERIOR TRIM

The overhang of a pitched roof that extends beyond the exterior walls of a house is called an eave, or cornice, which is shown in Figure 6.10. The cornice is composed of the soffit, the frieze board, the facia board, and the extended rafters. The frieze board is the exterior wood-trim board used to finish the exterior wall between the top of the siding or masonry and the eave, or overhang, of the roof framing. The facia board is an exterior wood trim used along the line of the end of the rafters where the roof overhangs the structural walls. The overhang of the cornice provides a decorative touch to the exterior of a house as well as some protection from the sun and rain.

ROOF COVERINGS

The roof is a key design element as well as a barrier against rain and snow. It is composed of a moisture-resistant felt underlayment or base, topped with a surface material. There is a wide variety of roofing materials to choose from, including asphalt shingles, wood shingles and shakes, tile, metal, slate, and concrete.

Asphalt Shingles

Asphalt shingles are asphalt-soaked felt coated with mineral granules. Most houses are roofed with asphalt shingles. The most durable ones include fiberglass.

Figure 6.9 Roof Designs

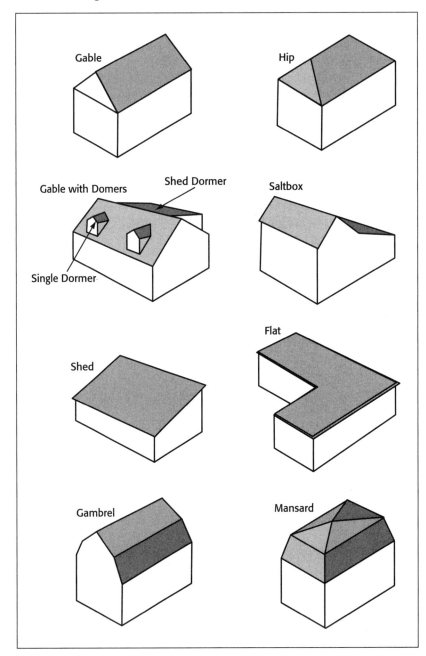

Figure 6.10 Eave or Cornice

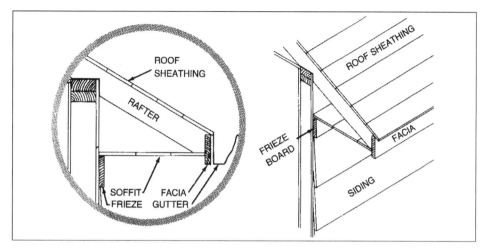

Numerous colors are available—even wood imitations. Asphalt is flame-resistant and can last 15 to 30 years, depending on the quality.

Wood Shingles and Shakes

Wood shingles are smooth; shakes are hand-split and rough and have a much more rustic appearance. Shingles and shakes are usually made from cedar, which naturally resists decay. They can be treated to maintain their natural color or left to weather to a silvery gray or light tan, depending on climatic conditions. Flammability is a drawback. Wood shingles and shakes can be treated with flame-resistant chemicals, but the process is expensive. Wood shingles and shakes are more expensive than asphalt shingles.

Clay or Concrete Tiles

Clay tiles are made in flat shingles, S shapes, and barrel shapes. They're most popular teamed with stucco exteriors to achieve a Spanish look. Clay tiles are durable enough to last a home's lifetime, but they require a stronger roof structure to support the additional weight.

Concrete tiles are lighter and less expensive than real clay, and they are easier to install. In fact, some varieties are light enough to be installed on a standard roof; that is, the roof framing would not have to be reinforced to withstand the weight. Imitations of real clay tiles, slate, wood shakes, and wood shingles all are available in concrete.

Slate

Slate shingles are among the most expensive roofing materials available, but they can last a home's lifetime and add to its market value. Like clay tiles, slate is quite heavy and may require extra strong framing for a house.

Metal

Metal is often aluminum, steel, or copper. It comes as shingles or as corrugated, ribbed, or flat strips. Metal can be painted, coated in vinyl-plastic, or natural. It is resistant to fire, but can be damaged by windblown objects. Aluminum can last 35 years; copper even longer.

Roll Roofing

Roll roofing is similar to asphalt shingles, but it comes in wide strips that are lapped horizontally. It is less expensive than many other forms of roofing and generally is used on shallow slopes because it has fewer places that would allow standing water to leak. Roll roofing generally won't last as long as shingles, however, and it's more prone to cracks, tears, and blisters.

EXTERIOR SIDING

Siding constitutes much of the decorative element of a home's exterior and is one of the main things a potential buyer will notice. It must look good and stand up to climatic conditions, too.

Real estate agents recognize the importance of the first impression a home creates and refer to it as *curb appeal.* The prospective buyer is attracted by the outside appearance of the house and grounds and is placed in a receptive mood, hoping to find other virtues inside the property that will reinforce the favorable first impression.

Exterior siding should be appropriate to the style of the house and should harmonize with its surroundings—the landscape and other homes in the neighborhood.

Solid Wood Siding

Solid lumber is the aristocrat of wood sidings. Cedar and redwood resist rot, so they can be left to weather. Other types of wood should be stained or painted.

Solid wood siding can last the lifetime of a house. A vapor barrier beneath the wood will prevent condensation from moisture inside the house that can rot wood and cause paint to peel.

Wood Shingles and Shakes

Wood shingles and shakes, made of cedar, cypress, or redwood, are naturally resistant to moisture and insect infestation. They don't require painting or staining except to change colors. Wood shingles have a smooth, uniform surface. Shakes are split and have a deeply textured face. Shingles and shakes are moderate to expensive in cost, depending on the grade of the wood.

Plywood Siding

Plywood siding is made of thin sheets of wood bonded together with waterproof adhesive. The outer veneer is available in about 75 wood species. Because plywood siding comes in large panels, installation is fast, and with fewer joints, air infiltration and noise are reduced.

Hardboard Siding

Hardboard is manufactured from wood fibers compressed into sheets. Hardboard surfaces range from smooth to textured and sometimes replicate wood grains. Hardboard siding is extremely durable and highly resistant to denting and gouging.

Aluminum Siding

Although aluminum siding has long been used to resurface older houses, in some areas it is now a strong competitor with wood and other materials on the exterior of new houses in all price classes. It is available with a baked-enamel or vinyl finish and is fireproof and virtually maintenance-free.

Aluminum siding should be backed with fiberboard or polystyrene foam to improve its insulating characteristics, to make it more dent-resistant, and to reduce the noise created by wind, rain, and hail.

Vinyl Siding

Vinyl siding is applied in much the same way as aluminum siding and is similar in appearance. Vinyl doesn't dent like aluminum does, however, and the color runs throughout the product, so chips and scratches are not easy to see. Because vinyl expands and contracts with temperature changes more than other materials, proper installation is important to avoid buckling or rippling.

Stucco

Stucco is a type of mortar that lends itself to Spanish-inspired architecture. It is noted for its durability, insulation, and resistance to fire, insects, and mildew.

Brick and Stone Veneers

Brick and stone veneers are expensive but can increase the market value of a home. They are popular because they are attractive, flame-resistant, and require little maintenance. Stonework is generally more costly than brickwork. Figure 6.11 shows a cutaway of a brick-veneered exterior wall, the most common type of masonry material used on houses.

Solid brick and stone are seldom used today as structural walls because of the expense involved. They require extra-thick foundation walls, and craftspeople able to install them are scarce.

Figure 6.11 Cutaway of Brick-Veneered Wall

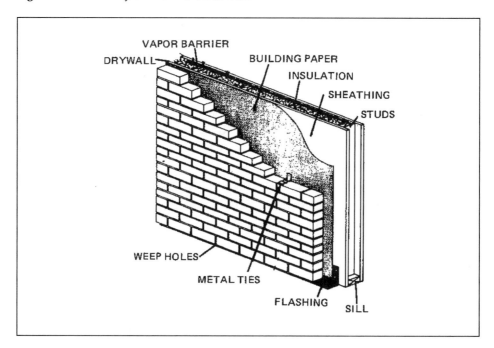

INSULATION

Properly insulating a home can reduce costly energy loss—helping the homeowner save on fuel bills during both the heating and cooling seasons. Fiberglass and rock wool are commonly used insulation materials. Figure 6.12 shows the four areas where home insulation is required. Insulation performance is rated in terms of R-value. (R means resistance to heat flow, the higher the R-value, the greater the insulating power.)

How much R-value is needed? The minimum R-value recommendations of the U.S. Department of Energy (DOE) are specific to zip-code areas and take into account climate, heating and cooling needs, types of heating used, and energy prices. The guidelines cover insulation requirements for ceilings, floors, exterior walls, attics, and crawl spaces. Check with local authorities for the insulating needs in your area. The website of the Department of Energy, *www.doe.gov*, has useful information on energy-efficient products and programs.

Asbestos and Urea Formaldehyde

Two kinds of home insulation to avoid using are asbestos and urea formaldehyde. Asbestos insulation, installed in the ceilings and walls of older homes, no longer

Figure 6.12 Areas That Require Insulation

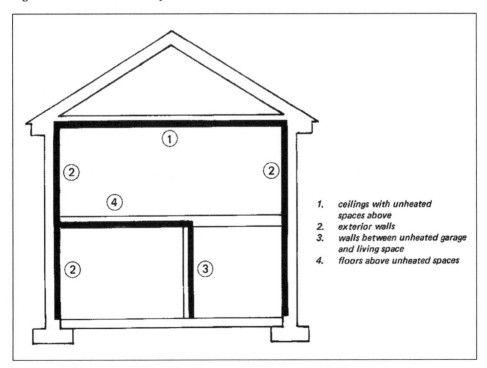

1. ceilings with unheated spaces above
2. exterior walls
3. walls between unheated garage and living space
4. floors above unheated spaces

is used because it is believed to cause cancer if its fibers get into the lungs. Urea formaldehyde may also be a potential health hazard, and its use is banned in the United States. It often emits noxious odors and toxic fumes, causing nausea and other irritations if inhaled. If you suspect a house has either asbestos or urea-formaldehyde insulation, consult a qualified inspector to examine all questionable areas.

EXTERIOR WINDOWS AND DOORS

Windows and doors contribute to the design and appearance of a house as well as provide a specific function. Skillfully placed doors regulate traffic patterns through the house and provide protection from intruders. Windows, in turn, admit light and a view of the outside.

Types of Windows

Figure 6.13 illustrates and describes the most common types of windows found in homes.

Energy-Efficient Windows

Because of dramatic improvements in the thermal performance of glass, along with improved window construction techniques, today's homeowner can save energy without sacrificing natural light and expansive views.

A standard energy rating, the R-value, measures window efficiency. The higher the R-value, the better the thermal efficiency. High-efficiency ratings are achieved largely through the use of low-emissivity (low-E) glass. Low-E refers to a number of glazing techniques that significantly improve the energy performance of glass. These include using double or triple panes, filling the air pockets between panes with argo gas, and using window films.

In addition, proper installation, weather stripping, and caulking are crucial. For example, a 1/16-inch crack around a three- by five-foot window is equivalent to having a brick-size hole in the wall.

Frames

There are four basic frame choices—wood, vinyl, fiberglass, and aluminum. Window frames made of wood are still viewed as the premium product. Wood frames, although good insulators, need paint and upkeep and can rot or warp (unless clad in vinyl or aluminum). Aluminum and vinyl windows, although good for upkeep, are poor insulators.

Figure 6.13 Common Window Types

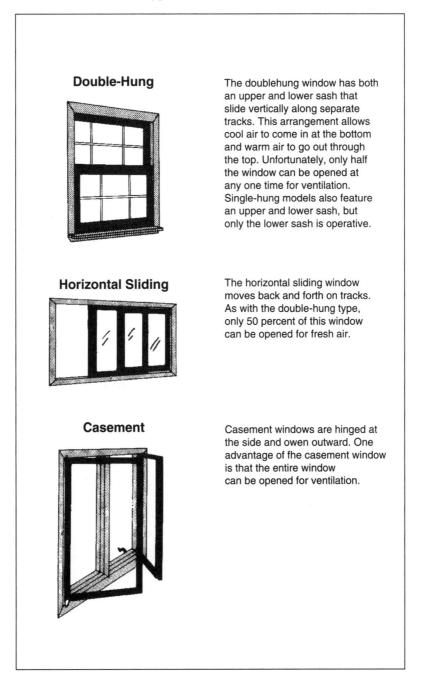

Double-Hung

The doublehung window has both an upper and lower sash that slide vertically along separate tracks. This arrangement allows cool air to come in at the bottom and warm air to go out through the top. Unfortunately, only half the window can be opened at any one time for ventilation. Single-hung models also feature an upper and lower sash, but only the lower sash is operative.

Horizontal Sliding

The horizontal sliding window moves back and forth on tracks. As with the double-hung type, only 50 percent of this window can be opened for fresh air.

Casement

Casement windows are hinged at the side and owen outward. One advantage of fhe casement window is that the entire window can be opened for ventilation.

Figure 6.13 *(Continued)*

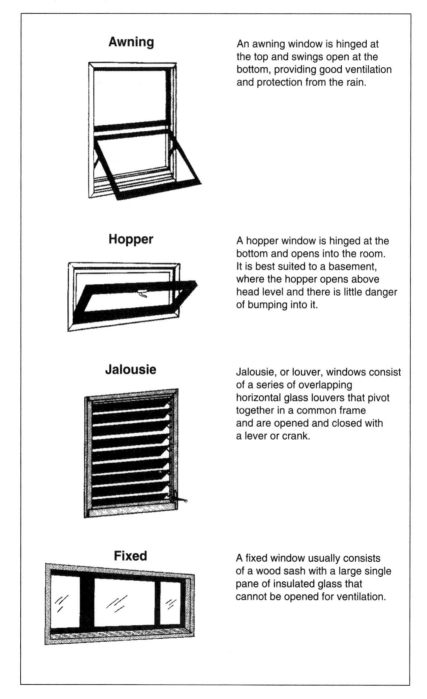

Awning

An awning window is hinged at the top and swings open at the bottom, providing good ventilation and protection from the rain.

Hopper

A hopper window is hinged at the bottom and opens into the room. It is best suited to a basement, where the hopper opens above head level and there is little danger of bumping into it.

Jalousie

Jalousie, or louver, windows consist of a series of overlapping horizontal glass louvers that pivot together in a common frame and are opened and closed with a lever or crank.

Fixed

A fixed window usually consists of a wood sash with a large single pane of insulated glass that cannot be opened for ventilation.

Fiberglass window frames are growing in popularity because they cost less than wood.

Noise Pollution

Windows can leak sound, just as pipes can leak water. Factors ranging from window design and materials to installation techniques affect the noise levels in homes. In general, though, energy-efficient windows cut down on the amount of sound entering a home.

Air absorbs sound and glass carries it. As a result, double- or triple-pane windows absorb more sound waves than do single-pane windows. Wood and vinyl frames absorb more sound than aluminum frames. In addition, applying soft materials such as foam or caulking around the frame will increase sound absorption even more.

Location of Exterior Doors

Exterior doors control passage in and out of the house. The main entrance door, usually the most attractive and most prominent door, should be located on the street side of the house. The goal is to create a good first impression and make the entry easy to find. The service door leads outside from rooms such as the kitchen, utility room, basement, or garage and is important for good traffic flow in the house. The patio door ties together indoors and outdoors and usually opens from a family room or dining area onto a patio, porch, or terrace.

An exterior door must be tight fitting, weather-stripped to prevent air leaks, and able to offer security against intruders.

Types of Doors

Doors are most often classified by construction and appearance. The four most common types are flush, panel, sliding glass, and storm and screen, which are shown in Figure 6.14.

Wood doors are available in solid wood (plank), veneer over solid wood, or veneer over a hollow core. Solid cores generally are preferred for exterior doors because they have better insulation qualities and are more resistant to warping. Hollow-core doors are lighter than the solid-core type and are used for interior locations, where heat and sound insulation are not so critical.

Steel and aluminum doors are not solid metal but have a lighter inner core of wood, wood and foam, or rigid foam. The aluminum or steel exterior surface comes primed or with a baked-enamel finish and doesn't swell or shrink. It's also weather-resistant and fire-retardant.

Figure 6.14 Types of Doors

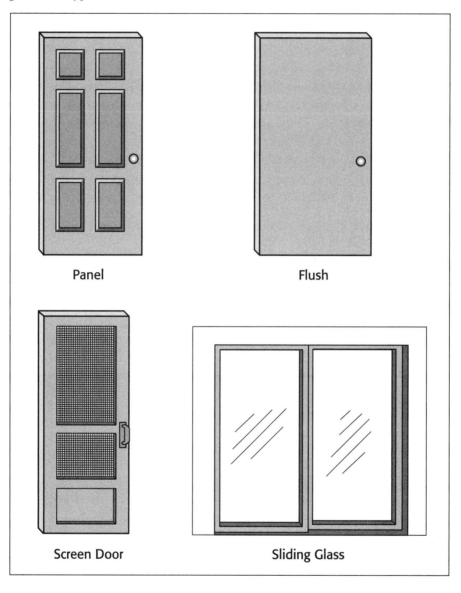

Sliding glass doors contain one or more panels that slide in a frame of metal or wood. The panels may hold either single-pane or insulating glass depending on the local climate. Some glass doors provide self-storing screens in a separate track of the door frame and some have inserts between glass panels that simulate the look of French doors.

Storm doors are made either with fixed glass panels, to improve weather resistance, or with both screen and glass inserts, to permit ventilation and insect control. In areas with moderate year-round temperatures, screen doors (without glass inserts) are frequently used. Combination doors combine the functions of both storm and screen doors with interchangeable glass and screen panels. Self-storing storm doors contain the equivalent of a two-track window, accommodating two inserts in one track and another in the adjacent track. The glass and screen inserts slide up and down just as they do in a vertical storm window.

Hollow-core doors are used for interior locations, where heat and sound insulation are not as critical.

INTERIOR WALLS AND FINISHING

Interior walls are the partitioning dividers for individual rooms and are usually covered with wallboard, although lath and plaster sometimes is used. The terms drywall and plasterboard are synonymous with wallboard. Wallboard is finished by a process known as taping and floating. Taping covers the joints between the sheets of wallboard. Floating is the process of smoothing out the walls by applying a plaster texture over the joints and rough edges where nails attach the wallboard to the wall studs. Texturing may be used in some areas as a final coating applied with a roller onto the wallboard prior to painting.

The final features added to a home include floor covering, trim, cabinetwork, and wall finishings of paint, wallpaper, or paneling.

Floor coverings of vinyl, wood (either in strips or blocks), carpet, brick, stone, or terrazzo tile are applied over the wood or concrete subflooring.

Trim masks the joints between the walls and ceiling and gives a finished decorator touch to the room. Trim, which is made of wood, hardboard, or vinyl, should be selected in a style that is complementary to the overall décor of the house.

Cabinetwork may be built on the job but is usually prefabricated in the mill. Cabinets should be well constructed to open and close properly and should conform to the style of the house.

Wall finishing is one of the most important decorator items in the home. Paint and wallpaper should be selected for both beauty and utility. Prefinished wood fiber and plastic panels such as polyethylene-covered plywood paneling now are widely used in less formal rooms. Either ceramic or plastic tiles are still used extensively as bathroom wall coverings.

PLUMBING

The plumbing system in a house is actually a number of separate systems, each designed to serve a special function. The water-supply system brings water to the house from the city main or from a well and distributes hot and cold water through two sets of pipes. The drainage system collects waste and used water from fixtures and carries it away to a central point for disposal outside the house. The vent-piping system carries out of the house all sewer gases that develop in drainage lines. It also equalizes air pressure within the waste system so that waste will flow away and not back up into the fixtures. The waste-collecting system is needed only when the main waste drain in the house is lower than the sewer level under the street or when the house has more than one drainage system. The house connection-pipe system, a single pipe, is the waste connection from the house to the city sewer line, to a septic tank, or to some other waste-disposal facility.

Plumbing must be installed subject to strict inspections and in accordance with local building codes, which dictate the materials to be used and the method of installation. Sewer pipes are made of cast iron, concrete, or plastic, while water pipes are made of copper, plastic, or galvanized iron. Recently, wrought-drawn copper and plastic have been used more frequently because they eliminate the need for piping joints in the foundation slab.

Plumbing Fixtures

Bathtubs, toilets, and sinks are made of vitreous china, enameled cast iron, enameled steel, stainless steel, or plastic. Plumbing fixtures have relatively long lives and are often replaced because of their obsolete style long before they have worn out.

Water Heaters

A water heater is basically an insulated metal tank that does just what its name implies. The size needed will depend on several factors including the number of people in the household, the hot water consumption during peak use periods (such as bathing or laundering), the recovery time required by the tank, and fuel costs in the area. Manufacturers recommend that the tank be placed closest to the point of use.

Water is almost always heated by gas or electricity. Water heaters are available in several capacities for residential use, ranging from 17 gallons up to 80 gallons. After water is heated to a predetermined temperature, the heater automatically shuts off. When hot water is drained off, cold water replaces it, and the heating unit turns on automatically. The newest systems are on-demand, which means that the water isn't heated until it is required.

HEATING AND AIR-CONDITIONING

Warm-air heating systems are most prevalent in today's houses. A forced warm-air system consists of a furnace, warm-air distributing ducts, and ducts for the return of cool air. All supply ducts should be well insulated and joints and other openings taped to prevent air leaks.

Each furnace has a capacity rated in British Thermal Units (BTUs). The number of BTUs given represents the furnace's heat output from gas, oil, or electric firing. A heating and cooling engineer can determine the cubic area of the house, as well as its construction, insulation, and window and door sizes. From this data, the engineer can compute the furnace capacity required to provide heat for the house in the coldest possible weather.

All gas pipes for heating and cooking are made of black iron. Gas pipes are installed in the walls or run overhead in the attic, where adequate ventilation is possible. They are never placed in the slab.

Almost all new homes today are centrally air conditioned. Air-conditioning units are rated either in BTUs or in tons. Twelve thousand BTUs are the equivalent of a one-ton capacity. An engineer can determine the measurements and problems inherent in the construction and layout of the space and from this information can specify the cooling capacity required to service the space or house adequately.

Combination heating and cooling systems are common in new homes. The most prevalent is the conventional warm-air heating system with a cooling unit attached. The same ducts and blower that force warm air are used to force cool air. The cooling unit is similar to a large air conditioner.

Many heating experts believe the heat pump will eventually replace today's conventional combination heating and cooling systems. The small heat pump is a single piece of equipment that uses the same components for heating or cooling. The most commonly used system for small heat pumps takes heat out of the ground or air in winter to warm the air in the house, and takes warm air out of the house in summer, replacing it with cooler air. The main drawback to the heat pump has been its initial cost. Once installed, however, it operates very economically and requires little maintenance. It works most efficiently in climates where winter weather is not severe, but new improvements make it adequate even in northern states.

Technical aspects of heating and air-conditioning should be handled by an experienced and qualified authority, although the homeowner should give due consideration to the operation and maintenance of the unit. Filters should be cleaned or replaced regularly and return air grilles and registers should be clear and clean for passage of the circulating air. The thermostat controls should be completely understood and properly set. The compressor and fan motors should be cared for on a regular maintenance schedule.

Solar Heating

The increased demand for fossil fuels has forced builders to look for new sources of energy. One of the most promising sources of heat for residential buildings is solar energy. The two methods for gathering solar energy are passive and active. The simplest form of solar heating is a passive system in which windows on the south side of a house take advantage of winter sunlight. A passive system can be improved inside the house by using water-filled containers, which are warmed by the sun during the day, to reradiate warmth into the room during the night. Such a system takes up space inside the home, however, and is not compatible with most decorating schemes. If these considerations are unimportant, and if there is adequate available sunlight, a passive solar heating system can be installed easily and at low cost.

Most solar heating units suitable for residential use are active systems that operate by gathering the heat from the sun's rays with one or more solar collectors, as shown in Figure 6.15. Water or air is forced through a series of pipes in the solar collector to be heated by the sun's rays. The hot air or water is then stored in a heavily insulated storage tank until it is needed to heat the house.

On a related note, solar heaters for swimming pools continue to provide a low-cost way of heating pool water. Solar pool heaters, in fact, constitute the largest single use for solar equipment.

Figure 6.15   Active Solar Water-Heating System

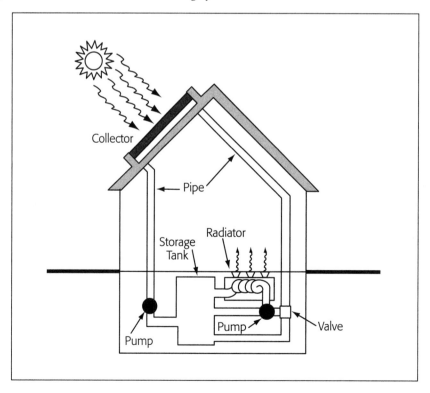

The U.S. government is one of the best sources on solar topics—whether for general information, the names of companies or organizations in the business, the names of architects familiar with solar design, or suggested references for further study.

ELECTRICAL SYSTEM

A good residential electrical system must have three important characteristics. First, it must meet all National Electrical Code (NEC) safety requirements: Each major appliance should have its own circuit, and lighting circuits should be isolated from electrical equipment that causes fluctuations in voltage. Second, the system must meet the home's existing needs and must have the capacity to accommodate room additions and new appliances. Finally, it should be convenient; there should be enough switches, lights, and outlets located so that occupants will not have to walk in the dark or use extension cords.

Electrical service from the power company is brought into the home through the transformer and the meter into a circuit breaker box (or a fused panel in older homes). The circuit breaker box is the distribution panel for the many electrical circuits in the house. In case of a power overload, the heat generated by the additional flow of electrical power will cause the circuit breaker to open at the breaker box, thus reducing the possibility of electrical fires. The architect or the builder is responsible for adhering to local building codes, which regulate electrical wiring. All electrical installations are inspected by the local building authorities, which assures the homeowner of the system's compliance with the building codes.

Residential wiring circuits are rated by the voltage that they are designed to carry. In the past, most residences were wired only for 110-volt capacity. Today, because of the many built-in appliances in use, 220- to 240-volt service is generally necessary. Amperage, the strength of a current expressed in amperes, is shown on the circuit breaker panel. The circuit breaker panel (or fuse panel) should have a capacity of at least 100 amperes. A larger service (150 to 200 or more amperes) may be needed if there is electric heat or an electric range or if the house has more than 3,000 square feet. New wiring will be required if the existing board's capacity is only 30 to 60 amperes. If there are fewer than 8 or 10 circuits, it will probably be necessary to add more. Each circuit is represented by a separate circuit breaker or fuse. A house with a lot of electrical equipment may require 15 to 20 or more circuits.

The construction checklist in the Appraisal Worksheet is a guideline to help you inspect the construction features and concepts that were covered in this chapter.

APPRAISAL WORKSHEET

External Inspection	
____1.	*Grading.* Be sure the ground around the foundation slopes away from the house. Look for signs of erosion or standing water in the yard.
____2.	*Foundation.* Make sure there are no serious cracks in the foundation or signs of uneven settling. Be sure the foundation's drainage system will direct water away from the house. Check that a nondeteriorating vapor barrier has been installed below the slab so that moisture will not creep through into the finished structure.
____3.	*Roof.* Shingles should be flat and secure. Check to see that flashing is in place around the chimney and where roof edges meet walls. Gutters and downspouts should be held securely in place. Splash blocks should carry water away from the house. Check the eaves for signs of rot or decay.
____4.	*Siding.* Note the type (wood, stucco, masonry, aluminum, vinyl) and condition of the siding. Check wood siding for bubbled or flaking paint, which may mean that the house has insufficient vapor-barrier protection. Probe wood siding for rot, especially the bottom boards along the foundation. Note bulges or cracks in stucco; deteriorating mortar between bricks or stones as well as breakdown of the bricks; and dents, chips, or cracks in aluminum or vinyl siding. Check the trim around the doors and windows and at the corners of the house. It should be firmly in place and well caulked. There should be a tight seal where siding meets chimney masonry.
Interior Inspection	
____1.	*Basement and attic.* Check for any indication of dampness or leaks in the basement. Look for cracks in foundation walls and in basement floors. Look over all exposed components (floor joists, support columns, insulation, electrical wiring, heating ducts, and plumbing) for obvious defects and improper workmanship. Check inside the attic for leaks. Carefully look over each rafter. Use a screwdriver to poke any suspicious looking spots for possible wood rot.
____2.	*Doors and windows.* Open and shut all windows and doors to make sure they operate properly and seal tightly. Check for broken or cracked glass in windows. Make sure there are no holes in the screens. Check that both windows and doors are weather-stripped.
____3.	*Floors.* Walk across all floors to check for squeaks. Carpet should be in reasonably good shape and should be tightly stretched with nearly invisible seams. Check for ridges or seam gaps in vinyl tile or sheet flooring. The finish of wood floors should be smooth and even.
____4.	*Finishes.* Check paint and varnish finishes in all rooms, including closets and stairways. Check the condition of wallpaper and paneling. Make sure all trim and molding is in place.
____5.	*Equipment.* Try all faucets and plumbing fixtures, including toilets, tubs, and showers. Turn on all heating-cooling and water-heating units to make sure that they operate properly. Check the draft and the damper on fireplaces. Check equipment, such as the intercom system, garage door opener, and doorbell. Make sure kitchen appliances are operable.

Figure 6.16 Anatomy of a House

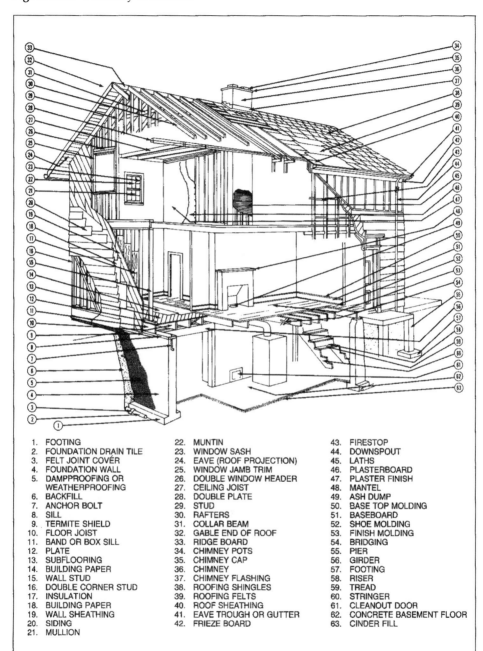

1. FOOTING	22. MUNTIN	43. FIRESTOP
2. FOUNDATION DRAIN TILE	23. WINDOW SASH	44. DOWNSPOUT
3. FELT JOINT COVER	24. EAVE (ROOF PROJECTION)	45. LATHS
4. FOUNDATION WALL	25. WINDOW JAMB TRIM	46. PLASTERBOARD
5. DAMPPROOFING OR WEATHERPROOFING	26. DOUBLE WINDOW HEADER	47. PLASTER FINISH
	27. CEILING JOIST	48. MANTEL
6. BACKFILL	28. DOUBLE PLATE	49. ASH DUMP
7. ANCHOR BOLT	29. STUD	50. BASE TOP MOLDING
8. SILL	30. RAFTERS	51. BASEBOARD
9. TERMITE SHIELD	31. COLLAR BEAM	52. SHOE MOLDING
10. FLOOR JOIST	32. GABLE END OF ROOF	53. FINISH MOLDING
11. BAND OR BOX SILL	33. RIDGE BOARD	54. BRIDGING
12. PLATE	34. CHIMNEY POTS	55. PIER
13. SUBFLOORING	35. CHIMNEY CAP	56. GIRDER
14. BUILDING PAPER	36. CHIMNEY	57. FOOTING
15. WALL STUD	37. CHIMNEY FLASHING	58. RISER
16. DOUBLE CORNER STUD	38. ROOFING SHINGLES	59. TREAD
17. INSULATION	39. ROOFING FELTS	60. STRINGER
18. BUILDING PAPER	40. ROOF SHEATHING	61. CLEANOUT DOOR
19. WALL SHEATHING	41. EAVE TROUGH OR GUTTER	62. CONCRETE BASEMENT FLOOR
20. SIDING	42. FRIEZE BOARD	63. CINDER FILL
21. MULLION		

The Sales Comparison Approach

7

Let's review briefly the three ways to form an opinion of real estate value:

1. With the cost approach, the appraiser calculates the cost of building a comparable structure on a similar site.

2. Using the income approach, the appraiser computes value based on the rental income the property is capable of producing.

3. Applying the sales comparison approach, the appraiser compares the property with others similar to it that have been sold recently.

The sales comparison approach is the most widely used method of valuing residential property and is the approach that will be covered in this chapter.

BASICS OF THE SALES COMPARISON APPROACH

In the sales comparison approach, the appraiser collects, classifies, analyzes, and interprets market data to determine the most probable selling price of a property.

The sales comparison approach requires the appraiser to do the following:

1. Identify the sources of value or characteristics of the subject property that would produce market demand. This takes into account the viewpoint of the typical buyer.

2. Find recently sold comparable properties that are reasonable alternatives for the typical buyer. (The appraiser also considers asking prices of properties currently being marketed for a possible indication of a market downturn.)

3. Compare the comparable properties to the subject property and adjust for differences.

4. Reach a final conclusion of value as of the indicated date.

Following is the formula for the sales comparison approach:

$$\text{Sales Price of Comparable Property} \pm \text{Adjustments}$$
$$= \text{Indicated Value of Subject Property}$$

The sales comparison approach is based on the principle of substitution; that is, the value of a property tends to equal the cost of acquiring a comparable property on the open market. This is just one of the principles that helps determine the value of a property.

Data for Sales Comparison Approach

When using the sales comparison approach, data is collected on sales of comparable properties. Only properties that have been sold within the past six months should be considered. They must have been arm's-length transactions, and the properties sold must be substantially similar to the subject property.

APPRAISAL PROCESS

Figure 3.2 on page 38 shows the process the appraiser follows when carrying out an assignment. If the steps in this flowchart are followed carefully, all the necessary information will be collected to arrive at an accurate appraisal. The process begins with a definition of the problem or assignment and ends with the final opinion of value.

APPLYING THE SALES COMPARISON APPROACH

Now let's follow the progress of a typical home appraisal using the sales comparison approach.

The subject property is a seven-room, brick, ranch-type house in a close-in suburban neighborhood. The appraiser's job is form an opinion of its market value.

The key to an accurate appraisal lies in methodical data collection. Much of the general data about the nation, region, and city can be found in the appraiser's own files and will take little fieldwork to gather. Let's assume that this general type of information has already been collected and that the appraiser is ready to begin the analysis at the neighborhood level. Neighborhood data is the only type of general information that will necessitate conducting significant fieldwork.

Neighborhood Data and Analysis

The value of a property can be influenced greatly by its surroundings. That's why it is important to analyze the neighborhood. Here are some other reasons:

- The neighborhood is the immediate environment of the subject—and no property can have a value higher than that set by its neighborhood.

- Lacking sales in the immediate neighborhood, it may be necessary to collect information on sales in reasonably comparable neighborhoods—and the appraiser needs the data on which to base comparisons.

- Neighborhood data provides background information. This is especially important if the appraisal report is to be submitted to someone who is not familiar with the area in which the subject property is located.

The appraiser can gather neighborhood information most systematically by using a form such as the one shown in Figure 7.1. This form contains all the basic data needed for a residential appraisal report.

Armed with the Neighborhood Data Form and a subdivision map of the area, similar to the one shown in Figure 7.2, the appraiser is ready for the field phase of the operation. This includes driving through the streets of the area, as well as checking background facts with banks, brokers, city hall, and other sources.

Neighborhood Boundaries

A neighborhood has a distinct identity. Several factors set a neighborhood apart from surrounding areas. Neighborhood boundaries are often established by natural barriers, such as rivers, lakes, and hills, or by man-made barriers, such as streets, highways, and rail lines. Boundaries may also be created by differences in land use, the average value of homes, city limits, census tracts, political divisions, school districts, and other factors.

Figure 7.2 shows that the subject neighborhood is bounded on the west by Osceola Avenue, which separates the single-family subject neighborhood from park district land and multifamily residences. Damper Boulevard is the eastern boundary and the point at which land use changes from residential to commercial. Tingley Road is the southern boundary because it separates the subject neighborhood from an area of larger, older but more expensive homes. A small lake on the north side of Bayshore Drive forms a physical barrier.

Figure 7.1 Neighborhood Data Form

NEIGHBORHOOD DATA FORM

BOUNDARIES: ADJACENT TO:

    NORTH _Osceola Avenue_   _small lake_

    SOUTH _Damper Beulevard_   _expensive homes_

    EAST _Bayshore Drive_   _commercial area_

    WEST _Tingley Road_   _Park District land and multifamily residences_

TOPOGRAPHY: _flat; gently slopes to street_   ☐ URBAN ☒ SUBURBAN ☐ RURAL

STAGE OF LIFE CYCLE OF NEIGHBORHOOD:

☐ GROWTH ☒ EQUILIBRIUM ☐ DECLINE ☐ REVITALIZATION

% BUILT UP: _98%_ GROWTH RATE: ☐ RAPID ☐ SLOW ☒ STEADY

AVERAGE MARKETING TIME: _5 mos._ PROPERTY VALUES: ☒ INCREASING ☐ DECREASING ☐ STABLE

SUPPLY/DEMAND: ☐ OVERSUPPLY ☐ UNDERSUPPLY ☒ BALANCED

CHANGE IN PRESENT LAND USE: _none anticipated_

POPULATION: ☐ INCREASING ☐ DECREASING ☒ STABLE AVERAGE FAMILY SIZE: _4_

AVERAGE FAMILY INCOME _$30,000 to $40,000_ INCOME LEVEL: ☒ INCREASING ☐ DECREASING

TYPICAL PROPERTIES:	% OF	AGE	PRICE RANGE	% OWNER OCCUPIED	% RENTALS
VACANT LOTS	2				
SINGLE-FAMILY RESIDENCES	98	10 yrs.	$105,000 to $135,00	97	3
2-6-UNIT APARTMENTS	0				
OVER 6-UNIT APARTMENTS	0				
NONRESIDENTIAL PROPERTIES	0				

TAX RATE: _$6 per $100 assessed value_ ☐ HIGHER ☐ LOWER ☒ SAME AS COMPETING AREAS

SPECIAL ASSESSMENTS OUTSTANDING: _none_   EXPECTED: _none_

SERVICES: ☒ POLICE ☒ FIRE ☒ GARBAGE COLLECTION   OTHER: _____

DISTANCE AND DIRECTION FROM

    BUSINESS AREA: _within 3 miles_

    COMMERCIAL AREA: _within 1 mile_

    PUBLIC ELEMENTARY AND HIGH SCHOOLS: _both within 1/2 mile_

    PRIVATE ELEMENTARY AND HIGH SCHOOLS: _elementary, 2 miles; high school, 1 mile_

    RECREATIONAL AND CULTURAL AREAS: _within 3 miles_

    EXPRESSWAY INTERCHANGE: _within 3 miles, in business area_

    PUBLIC TRANSPORTATION: _bus–good service_

        TIME TO REACH BUSINESS AREA: _15 min._ COMMERCIAL AREA: _5 min._

    EMERGENCY MEDICAL SERVICE: _20 min._

GENERAL TRAFFIC CONDITIONS: _good_

PROXIMITY TO HAZARDS (AIRPORT, CHEMICAL STORAGE, ETC.): _none nearby_

PROXIMITY TO NUISANCES (SMOKE. NOISE, ETC): _none nearby_

Life Cycle

A residential neighborhood is constantly undergoing changes in its life cycle. The life of a neighborhood usually involves the following three stages:

1. Growth—the period during which the neighborhood is being built up.

2. Equilibrium—the period of stability when new building has virtually stopped and houses in the neighborhood are usually at their highest monetary level.

3. Decline—the period during which the aging housing stock requires increased maintenance, which it may not receive, with the result that the neighborhood enters a period of diminishing value and desirability.

Figure 7.2 Subdivision Map

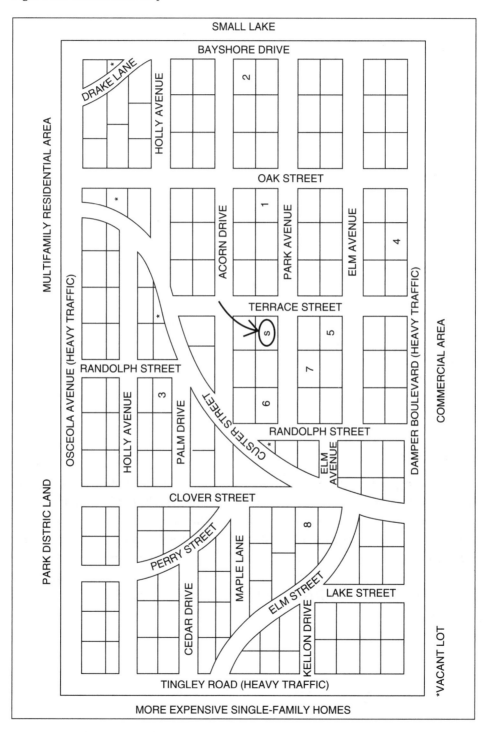

These stages obviously take a long time to develop and may be followed by a period of renewal and rehabilitation, at which point the cycle tends to repeat.

The lots on the subdivision map shown in Figure 7.2 that are marked with an asterisk are vacant. New building has practically stopped, indicating that this neighborhood is perhaps in the stage of equilibrium.

To complete the Neighborhood Data Form, appraisers use a number of different sources. These may include the appraiser's own files, county or city records, brokers, banks, lawyers, homeowners, merchants, published records, and field observations.

Site Data and Analysis

After all the background data on the neighborhood has been gathered, the appraiser can begin to collect information about the property under appraisal. To form an opinion of the value of improved real estate, the appraiser gathers and analyzes data on each of the two physical components of the property—the site and the house. The site will be examined first.

The rectangular lot is 80 by 150 feet—a typical size in the neighborhood. The lot slopes gently toward the street. It is evident that the owner has spent a good deal of time on landscaping, resulting in a pleasant balance between trees and shrubs.

All important information about the site is recorded on a Site Data Form, similar to the one shown in Figure 7.3. The appraiser probably had to check with a number of sources to find all of the required information.

Building Data and Analysis

The house inspection is next. The exterior walls are face brick with wood trim. The roof is a simple gable type made of asphalt shingles with gutters all around. Once the exterior of the house has been examined, an interior inspection must be made. A room-by-room analysis can be conducted most systematically by using a Building Data Form, such as the one in Figure 7.4. Remember, the appraiser will have to select and screen comparable properties to apply the sales comparison approach. Accuracy will depend, to a large extent, on how diligently information is gathered on the subject house.

Figure 7.3 Site Data Form

SITE DATA FORM

ADDRESS: _____ 155 Park Avenue, Anytown, USA _____

LEGAL DESCRIPTION: _____ Lot 15, Pine Valley Estate, Section 10 _____

_____

_____

_____

_____

DIMENSIONS: __ 80' X 150' _____

SHAPE: __ rectangular _____ SQUARE FEET: 12,000 _____

TOPOGRAPHY: Level-slopes to Street _ VIEW: __ Street-typical _____

NATURAL HAZARDS: _none _____

    ☐ INSIDE LOT   ☒ CORNER LOT   ☐ FRONTAGE _80'_____

ZONING: _Residential _____ ADJACENT AREAS: __Other residential __

UTILITIES: ☒ ELECTRICITY   ☒ GAS   ☒ WATER   ☒ TELEPHONE

           ☒ SANITARY SEWER   ☒ STORM SEWER

IMPROVEMENTS: DRIVEWAY: _asphalt_   STREET: _asphalt_

           SIDEWALK: _concrete_ CURB/GUTTER: _concrete_ ALLEY: _none___

           STREETLIGHTS: _yes___

LANDSCAPING: _well done with balance between the trees and shrubs _____

TOPSOIL: _good _____ DRAINAGE: _good _____

EASEMENTS: _easement running across rear 12 ft. of property _____

DEED RESTRICTION: _10 ft. to side property lines; 35 ft. to street; 60 ft. to rear property line_

SITE PLAT:

See the attached Subdivision Map.

Figure 7.4 Building Data Form

BUILDING DATA FORM

ADDRESS: _155 Park Avenue_

NO. OF UNITS: _____1_____ NO. OF STORIES: _____1_____ ORIENTATION: N S(E)W

TYPE: _Single-family_ DESIGN: _Ranch_ AGE: _10 years_ SQUARE FEET: _1,800_

	GOOD	FAIR	POOR
GENERAL CONDITION OF EXTERIOR	✓		
FOUNDATION TYPE _conc._(BSMT)/CRAWL SP./SLAB	✓		
EXTERIOR WALLS:(BRICK)/BLOCK/VENEER/STUCCO/	✓		
WOOD/COMPOSITE/ALUMINUM/VINYL	✓		
WINDOW FRAMES: METAL/(WOOD)	✓		
STORM WINDOWS: _alum_ SCREENS: _alum_	✓		
GARAGE: _brick_ (ATTACHED)/DETACHED	✓		
NUMBER OF CARS: _2_			
☐ PORCH ☐ DECK ☐ PATIO ☐ SHED			
OTHERS: _____	✓		
GENERAL CONDITION OF INTERIOR	✓		
INTERIOR WALLS:(DRYWALL)/PLASTER/WOOD	✓		
CEILINGS: _drywall_	✓		
FLOORS: (WOOD)/CONCRETE/(TILE)/(CARPET)	✓		
ELECTRICAL WIRING AND SERVICE: _220 volt_	✓		
HEATING PLANT: _forced-air_ AGE: _10 yrs._			
(GAS)/OIL/WOOD/ELECTRIC	✓		
CENTRAL AIR-CONDITIONING: _yes_ AIR FILTRATION: ____	✓		
NUMBER OF FIREPLACES: _1_ TYPE: _masonry_	✓		
OTHER _____	✓		
BATHROOM: FLOOR _cer. tile_ WALLS _cer.tile paint_ FIXTURES _vanity, tab, shower, tiolet_	✓		
BATHROOM: FLOOR _same_ WALLS _same_ FIXTURES _same as above_	✓		
BATHROOM: FLOOR___ WALLS___ FIXTURES ___	✓		
KITCHEN: FLOOR _vinyl tile_ WALLS___ CABINETS _wood_	✓		
FIXTURES _double stainless steel sink, ref. dishwasher, range w/head + exhaust._	✓		

ROOM SIZES	LIVING ROOM	DINING ROOM	KITCHEN	BEDROOM	BATH	CLOSETS	FAMILY ROOM
BASEMENT							
1ST FLOOR	①	①	①	③	②	⑤	①
2ND FLOOR							
ATTIC							

DEPRECIATION (DESCRIBE):

PHYSICAL DETERIORATION _House is 10 years old; normal wear and tear._

FUNCTIONAL OBSOLESCENCE _None_

EXTERNAL OBSOLESCENCE _None_

Comparable Sales Data and Analysis

With all the pertinent background information on the subject property and its neighborhood, the appraiser is ready to begin the most critical part of the appraisal—gathering comparable sales data to use in applying the sales comparison approach.

A comparable property (comp) must meet three conditions:

1. It must be reasonably similar to the subject property. This simply means that detailed site and building data on the comp is collected so that the relevant features of the subject property can be compared with the same features of the comp.

2. A comp must be a relatively recent sale. A sale made a year or two before the appraisal will most likely not reflect current market value.

3. The sale must be an arm's-length transaction. This means that the following guidelines have been met:

   ■ The property was offered for sale on the open market.

   ■ There was a reasonable time allowed to sell.

   ■ The buyer and seller both acted with knowledge of the property's features, including disclosure of property defects known by the seller.

   ■ No pressure (such as a forced sale) was brought on either party to the sale.

There are many ways to acquire information about recent property sales—some more reliable than others. Many Internet sites publish information from public records and some even offer "appraisals" based on that data. Unfortunately, the information may come from an assessor's office and reflect assessed value rather than market value; information based on actual sales is more reliable. Some sites use sales data, but don't define neighborhood boundaries accurately. Following are the best resources for an appraiser:

■ Records in the appraiser's own office

■ Official records of deeds in the county clerk's or assessor's office. A deed will list the parties to the sale, date of sale, legal description of the property, and any encumbrances. Transfer tax stamps will indicate a value, though these also can be used to misrepresent the actual transaction price.

■ Brokers and sales agents involved in the sale. The multiple listing system (MLS) will indicate sold listings.

- Either the buyer or seller—the principals to the transaction. The buyer or seller can tell the appraiser the price paid for the home as well as any special considerations or motivation surrounding the sale. For example, a person anticipating a foreclosure might sell a property for less than he or she would under normal circumstances. The selling price in such a case would not reflect the property's true market value.

- Published records of sales, though sales data listed in newspapers may be unreliable and should always be verified

In any list of sales that is prepared, it is likely that several sales will have to be eliminated. Following are some of the more common reasons for rejecting a sale:

- The sale was a foreclosure.

- The parties to the sale were related individuals or corporations.

- Either party was under some compulsion to enter into the sale.

- The sale was made to liquidate assets for estate tax purposes.

- The sale was affected by exceptional terms, either all cash or little or no cash.

- The sale was too long ago. Sales made several years before the appraisal should not be used unless they are the only ones available or unless property values have undergone little or no change.

- The sale was not an arm's-length transaction for any reason at all.

A sale made under any of these conditions may not reflect the property's true market value. The important thing to remember is that if you are doubtful about the validity of a sale *for any reason,* you should eliminate it from your list of sales.

Comparison Chart

The Comparable Sales Chart in Figure 7.5 lists the common significant property variables that warrant price adjustments. The chart provides space to describe the subject property and its comparables and space to adjust the sales price of each comparable to account for significant property differences.

The subject property and each comparable should be identified by street address. The proximity of each comparable to the subject property should also be noted to determine whether a value adjustment will be made for location. The sales price of each comparable as well as the source of the market data used should be recorded. The easiest way to complete the chart is to describe all the details of the subject property, then do the same for each comparable in turn.

The categories listed on the Comparable Sales Chart under "Value Adjustments" produce the greatest effect on value in standard residential appraisals. These include the following:

- *Sales or financing concessions.* Describe any financing arrangements that you are aware of, such as mortgage assumptions, buydowns, installment sales contracts, and wraparound loans, that may have affected the sales price of a comparable property.

- *Adjusted value.* Add or subtract any difference in value warranted by changes in the market since the sale of the comparable property.

- *Date of sale.* An adjustment will probably be necessary for a sale made six months or more before the date of the appraisal. Have housing prices increased, decreased, or stayed the same?

- *Location.* The comparable property should be in the same neighborhood as the subject property. (The appraiser may have no recourse except to use properties outside the immediate area if few sales have been made in the neighborhood or if the subject property is in a rural area.) Within the same neighborhood, locations can offer significant variances, such as proximity to different land uses or frontage on a heavily traveled street. A property located across the street from a park would tend to be more valuable than one located adjacent to a highway.

- *Site/view.* The size of the lot should be given and the site rated as good, fair, or poor on the basis of physical features as well as on view.

  Site adjustments may reflect differences in size, shape, topography, landscaping, drainage, streets, sidewalks, or other features. Except for irregularities that would make parts of a lot unusable, impair privacy, or restrict on-site parking, differences in street frontage and total square footage are the most important considerations. Trees and other plantings should be of the same maturity as those of the subject property and of approximately the same quantity and quality.

  In most neighborhoods, view adjustments are uncommon; however, adjustments for houses with open space, a golf course, water, or mountain views may be very substantial.

- *Design and appeal.* The style of a house probably should follow the rule of conformity; that is, the design should be compatible with that of others in the neighborhood. This doesn't mean that all of the homes should reflect a cookie-cutter similarity, but that they should be alike in size, placement on the property, and quality of construction and finishing materials.

- *Quality of construction.* If not the same as or equivalent to the subject property, the quality of construction of the comp will be a major adjustment. Available comparables within a particular builder's subdivision typically will be of the same construction quality. Building-cost estimating guides, published to assist builders (and appraisers, as you will learn in Chapter 9), can be used to rate construction quality in a range from low to excellent.

- *Age.* Because most subdivisions are completed within a relatively short period of time, there may be no significant differences among comparables due to the age of the improvements. A brand-new home would likely be valued by the builder according to actual costs, overhead, and profit. With older homes in good general condition, an age difference of five years in either direction is usually not significant. Overall upkeep is of greater importance, although the age of the house may alert the appraiser to look for outmoded design or fixtures or any needed repairs.

- *Condition.* The overall condition of each property will be noted as good, fair, or poor. An adjustment would be indicated if the comparable is in better or worse condition than the subject property.

- *Above-grade room count.* The total number of rooms in the house, excluding bathrooms and any basement (below-grade) rooms, is listed here. The number of bedrooms and baths and the total above-grade square footage are also noted. A major adjustment is needed if the subject property has fewer than three bedrooms and the comparables all have at least three, or vice versa. The total number of full baths (sink, toilet, and tub/shower), three-quarter baths (sink, toilet, and shower), and half-baths (sink and toilet) are tallied in this category. Modern plumbing is assumed, with an adjustment made for out-of-date fixtures.

- *Basement and finished rooms below grade.* The appraiser should note any below-grade improvements, such as a finished basement.

- *Functional utility.* The house's overall compatibility with its intended use, as defined in the marketplace, should be noted. This category includes design features, such as layout and room size, that are currently desirable. In some areas, an enclosed patio (the "Arizona" room or "Florida" room) is an expected feature. In cold-weather areas, a basement is appreciated for its insulating and storage benefits.

- *Heating/cooling.* The appraiser notes the type of heating unit and air-conditioning system, if any, of the subject and the comparables.

- *Garage/carport.* If the subject property does not have a garage, any garage on a comparable property would require an adjustment. A garage on the

Figure 7.5 Comparable Sales Chart

	SUBJECT	COMPARABLE NO. 1	+(-)$ Adjustment	COMPARABLE NO. 2	+(-)$ Adjustment	COMPARABLE NO. 3	+(-)$ Adjustment	COMPARABLE NO. 4	+(-)$ Adjustment	COMPARABLE NO. 5	+(-)$ Adjustment
Address	155 Terrace Street	167 Oak Ave.		180 Bayshore Dr.		205 Randolph St.		500 Damper St.		127 Terrace St.	
Proximate to Subject		Within half-mile		Within half-mile		Within half-mile		Within half-mile		Within half-mile	
Sales Price		$110,000		$124,400		$111,500		$100,000		$114,000	
Data Source	owner	sales agent		sales agent		sales agent		sales agent		sales agent	
VALUE ADJUSTMENTS	Description	Description		Description		Description		Description		Description	
Sales or Financing Concessions	NA	none		none		none		none		none	
Adjusted Value		$		$		$		$		$	
Date of Sale/Time	NA	1 yr. ago	+4,600	2 mos. ago		4 mos. ago		3 mos. ago		1 mo. ago	
Adjusted Value		$		$		$		$		$	
Location	qult st.	qult st.		facing lake	-10,000	qult st.		heavy traffic		qult st.	
Site/View	80' x 150' good	75' x 150' good		85' x 150'/gd.		80' x 150'/gd.		75' x 145'/poor*	-2,700	80' x 150'/gd.	
Design and Appeal	Ranch/good	Ranch/good		Ranch/good		Ranch/good		Ranch/good		Ranch/good	
Quality of Construction	Brick/good	Brick/good		Brick/good		Brick/good		Brick/good		Brick/good	
Age	10 yrs.	11 yrs.		10 yrs.		11 yrs.		10 yrs.		10 yrs.	
Condition	good	good		good		good		good		good	
Above Grade Room Count (Total/Bdrms/Baths)	7 / 3 / 2	7 / 3 / 2		7 / 3 / 2		7 / 3 / 2		7 / 3 / 2		7 / 3 / 2	
Gross Living Area	1,800 sq. ft.	1,175 sq. ft.		1,800 sq. ft.		1,750 sq. ft.		1,850 sq. ft.		1,800 sq. ft.	
Basement & Finished	full	full		full		full		full		full	
Room Below Grade	basement	basement		basement		basement		basement		basement	
Functional Utility	adequate	adequate		adequate		adequate		adequate		adequate	
Heating/Cooling	Central H/A	Central H/A		Central H/A		no air	+2,200	no air	+2,200	Central H/A	
Garage/Carport	2-car att.	2-car att.		2-car att.		2-car att.		2-car att.		2-car att.	
Other Ext. Improvements	none	none		none		none		none		none	
Special Energy Efficient Items	none										
Fireplace(s)	yes/1	yes/1		yes/1		yes/1		yes/1		yes/1	
Other Int. Improvements	none	none		none		none		none		none	
Add'l Adj		☒+ ☐- $4,600		☐+ ☒- $10,000		☒+ ☐- $2,200		☒+ ☐- $5,200		☐+ ☐- $-0-	
Adjusted Value		$114,600		$114,400		$113,700		$105,200		$114,000	

* The undesirable view of comp 4 is reflected in the adjustment for location. Note: All adjustments are rounded to the nearest $100.

	SUBJECT	COMPARABLE NO. 1		COMPARABLE NO. 2		COMPARABLE NO. 3		COMPARABLE NO. 4		COMPARABLE NO. 5	
Address	152 Randolph St.	250 Park Ave.		180 Bayshore Dr.		325 Clover St.					
Proximate to Subject											
Sales Price		$119,000		$109,000		$109,000					
Data Source		sales agent		sales agent		sales agent					
VALUE ADJUSTMENTS	Description	Description	+(-)$ Adjustment	Description	+(-)$ Adjustment	Description	+(-)$ Adjustment	Description	+(-)$ Adjustment	Description	+(-)$ Adjustment
Sales or Financing Concessions		none		none		none					
Adjusted Value		$		$		$		$		$	
Date of Sale/Time		5 mos. ago		4 mos. ago		6 mos. ago					
Adjusted Value		$		$		$		$		$	
Location		quit st.		quit st.		quit st.					
Site/View		80' x 150' good		75' x 155'/gd.		75' x 150'/gd.					
Design and Appeal		Ranch/good		Ranch/good		Ranch/good					
Quality of Construction		Brick/good		Frame/good	+3,600	Frame/good	+3,600				
Age		10 yrs.		11 yrs.		11 yrs.					
Condition		good		good		good					
Above Grade Room Count (Total / Bdrms / Baths)	Total / Bdrms / Baths	7 / 3 / 2½		7 / 3 / 2		7 / 3 / 2		Total / Bdrms / Baths		Total / Bdrms / Baths	
Gross Living Area	sq. ft.	1,750 sq. ft.	-3,260	1,800 sq. ft.		1,750 sq. ft.		sq. ft.		sq. ft.	
Basement & Finished		full basement		full basement		full basement					
Room Below Grade		adequate		adequate		adequate					
Functional Utility		adequate		adequate		adequate					
Heating/Cooling		Central H/A		Central H/A		no air	+2,200				
Garage/Carport		2-car att.		2-car att.		2-car att.					
Other Ext.		none		none		none					
Improvements		none		none		none					
Special Energy Efficient Items		yes/1		yes/1		yes/1					
Fireplace(s)		none		none		none					
Other Int. Improvements											
Add'l Adj.		☒+ ☐- $3,200		☐+ ☒- $3,600		☒+ ☐- $5,800		☐+ ☐-		☐+ ☐-	
Adjusted Value		$115,800		$112,600		$114,780					

subject property would be compared for the type of construction and size.

- *Other exterior improvements.* The porch, patio, pool, deck, or any other living or recreation area not part of the primary house area is included here.

- *Special energy-efficient items.* High R-factor insulation, solar heating units, or other energy-conservation features should be noted. As with all price adjustments, any made for energy-conservation features should reflect how much more the market will pay for the property because of the existence of the feature.

- *Fireplace(s).* The number and type of fireplaces should be recorded.

- *Other interior improvements.* An adjustment factor is indicated if either the subject property or one of the comparables has any other interior property improvement that adds to or subtracts from its value. Luxurious finishing, particularly in the kitchen and baths, could add to a home's value.

- *Additional adjustments.* Total the dollar amounts of the positive and negative adjustments, then enter the net value of each comparable and check the + or – box as appropriate. Very large adjustments suggest that the properties are not comparable.

- *Adjusted value.* The amount of any additional adjustment is added to or subtracted from the sales price of the comparable property to obtain an adjusted sales price. This is the appraiser's best opinion of what the comparable property would have sold for if it had possessed all the significant characteristics of the subject property.

The next several pages contain an examination of how the appraiser derived the dollar adjustment values that were applied to the comparable sales in Figure 7.5.

Adjustment Process

At this point, all the data the appraiser will need to arrive at a fair market value opinion of the subject property has been gathered. The next step is to compare properties and make adjustments where needed. Although adjustments may be made for some differences between the subject property and the comparables, most of the following factors should be similar:

- Style of house
- Age

- Number of rooms
- Number of bedrooms
- Number of bathrooms
- Size of lot
- Size of dwelling
- Terms of sale
- Type of construction
- General condition

Naturally, wherever differences exist, adjustments must be made to bring the comparable properties into conformity with the subject property. The four major categories in which adjustments for differences must be made are the following:

1. *Date of sale.* An adjustment must be made if market conditions change between the date of the sale of the comparable property and the date of the appraisal. Changes in market conditions may be caused by such things as fluctuations in supply and demand, inflation, and economic recession.

2. *Location.* An adjustment may be necessary to compensate for locational differences between comparables and the subject property. For example, similar properties might differ in price from neighborhood to neighborhood or even in more desirable locations within the same neighborhood.

3. *Physical features.* Physical features that may require adjustments include the age of the structure, the number of rooms, the layout of the rooms (functional utility), the square feet of living space, the exterior and interior condition, and the presence or absence of special features such as a garage, central air-conditioning, fireplace, swimming pool, energy-efficient items, and the like. Not every feature will add to the property's value. The swimming pool that is a desirable amenity in Florida may actually decrease the value of a home in Wisconsin.

4. *Terms and conditions of sale.* This consideration becomes important if a sale is not financed by a standard mortgage.

Comparable sales must be adjusted *to* the subject property. That is, the subject property is the standard against which the comparable sales are evaluated and adjusted. Thus, if a feature in the comparable property is superior to that in the subject property, a minus (−) adjustment is required to make that feature equal to that in the subject property. Conversely, if a feature in the comparable property is inferior to that in the subject property, a plus (+) adjustment is required to make the feature equal to that in the subject property.

Estimating the Dollar Value of Adjustments

The most difficult step when using the sales comparison approach is determining the dollar amount of each adjustment. The accuracy of an appraisal applying this approach depends on the appraiser's use of reliable adjustment values. The adjustment value of a property feature is not simply the cost to construct or add that feature but what a buyer is willing to pay for it, typically a lesser amount. An opinion of market value must always consider the demands of the marketplace.

Ideally, if properties could be found that were exactly alike except for one variable, the adjustment value of that variable would be the difference in selling prices of the two properties.

Example

House A is very similar to House B, except that House A has an attached garage and House B has a carport. House A sold for $220,000; House B for $210,000. Because the garage is the only significant difference between the two properties, its market value is likely to be the difference between the selling price of $220,000 and the selling price of $210,000, or $10,000.

This type of analysis is called matched-pair analysis or paired-data analysis. An adjustment supported by just one matched pair, as in the example, however, may be unreliable. In actual practice, the appraiser will analyze as many properties as needed to be able to isolate each significant variable and to substantiate the accuracy of an adjustment value.

The number of sales needed for an accurate estimate of market value cannot be easily specified, but the fewer the sales, the more carefully they must be investigated. If the appraiser analyzes 10 to 20 or more properties, a market pattern may be more evident and, with better documentation, the value of individual differences may be estimated fairly accurately.

Figure 7.6 is a Sales Price Adjustment Chart that has been completed for eight properties, all comparable to each other. Each relevant adjustment variable has been highlighted. An appraiser will ordinarily need two or more instances of each variable as a check on the accuracy of an adjustment value.

Because Properties A and C exhibit no variables, they will be used to define the standard against which the worth of each variable will be measured. Property A sold for $225,000 and Property C sold for $223,750. Because the selling prices are so close, $225,000 will be used as the base house value for a typical property in the neighborhood.

Now let's estimate how much each adjustment factor is worth in dollars as each one is analyzed singly. Sometimes, an adjustment is a percentage of the sales price, and at other times, the adjustment is a dollar value.

Time Adjustment

The time factor refers to the economic changes from the date of the sale to the date of the appraisal. To isolate the time factor, those sales that differ from each other in the date of sale only are selected. If several properties are alike except for the length of time since the date of sale, then it is logical to assume that the time factor is reflected in the difference in selling prices.

Property D was sold one year ago for $220,000 (see Figure 7.6). Property A, the base house, or standard, sold one month ago for $225,000. The adjustment value to be made in the case of a year-old sale is as follows:

$$\$225,000 - \$220,000 = \$5,000$$

The $5,000 adjustment value can be expressed as a percentage of the total cost of the property:

$$\frac{\$5,000}{\$220,000} = .0227, \text{ or rounded to } 2.3\%$$

In this case, the adjustment value of the variable is $5,000. If a one-year time adjustment was required for another property, the dollar value of the adjustment would be the amount derived by applying the percentage of value to that property's sales price.

Note that the adjustment values determined through matched-pair analysis in Figure 7.6 were applied to the comparable properties used in the sample appraisal in Figure 7.5. For example, the sales price of Property 1 was adjusted by 2.3 percent ($310,000 ×.023 = $7,130) because it was a year-old sale.

Location

Property G, on a more desirable site facing a small lake, sold for $10,900 *more* than the standard; therefore, this superior location indicates an adjustment of $10,900 (about 3.2 percent).

Property B, on the other hand, fronts on a heavily traveled street and is directly across from a commercial shopping area. Property B sold for $7,000 *less* than the base value house.

Physical Features

In the sample appraisal, physical feature adjustments were made for brick versus frame siding (Properties 7 and 8), an extra half-bath (4, 6), and central air-conditioning (3, 4, 8).

Based on the matched-pair analysis in Figure 7.6, the appraiser estimated the following adjustment values:

> brick over frame—$7,000 (Property E);
> extra half-bath—$3,000 (Property F);
> central air-conditioning—$2,200 (Property H)

These adjustment values were then applied to the appropriate properties in the sample appraisal.

Figure 7.6 Sales Price Adjustment Chart

	COMPARABLES									
	A	B	C	D	E	F	G	H		
SALES PRICE	$325,000	$318,000	$323,750	$320,000	$318,000	$328,000	$335,900	$322,800		
FINANCING	standard mortgage	standard mortgage	standard mortgage	standard mortgage	standard mortgage	standard mortgage	standard mortgage	standard mortgage		
DATE OF SALE	1 mo. 2 go	4 ms, 2 go	2 ms, 2 go	1 gr, 2go	3 mgs, 2go	5 mgs, 2 go	3 mgs, 2 go	2 mgs, 2 go		
LOCATION	quiet street	quiet street	quiet street	quiet street	quiet street	quiet street	quiet street	quiet street		
SITE/VIEW	good	good	good	good	good	good	good	good		
SIZE OF LOT	95' x 125'	95' x 125'	95' x 125'	78' x 130'	75' x 135'	15' x 125'	75' x 125'	80' x 120'		
DESIGN AND APPEAL	good	good	good	good	good	good	good	good		
CONSTRUCTION	brick	brick	brick	brick	frame siding	brick	brick	brick		
AGE	14 yrs.	14 yrs.	14 yrs.	14 yrs.	14 yrs.	14 yrs.	14 yrs.	14 yrs.		
CONDITION	good	good	good	good	good	good	good	good		
NO. OF RMS/BEDRMS/BATHS	8/3/2	8/3/2	8/3/2	8/3/2	8/3/2	8/3/2 ½	8/3/2	8/3/2		
SQ. OF LIVING SPACE	1,900	1,850	1,900	1,850	1,900	1,925	1,875	1,900		
OTHER SPACE (BASEMENT)	full basement	full basement	full basement	full basement	full basement	full basement	full basement	full basement		
FUNCTIONAL UTILITY	2 deg.	2 deg.	2 deg.	2 deg.	2 deg.	2 deg.	2 deg.	2 deg.		
HEATING/COOLING	central H/A	central H/A	central H/A	central H/A	central H/A	central H/A	central H/A	no central air		
GARAGE/CARPORT	2-car 2H	2-car 2H	2-car 2H	2-car 2H	2-car 2H	2-car 2H	2-car 2H	2-car 2H		
OTHER EXT. IMPROVEMENTS	patio	patio	patio	patio	patio	patio	patio	patio		
SPECIAL ENERGY-EFFICIENT ITEMS	none	none	none	none	none	none	none	none		
FIREPLACE(S)	yes/1	yes/1	yes/1	yes/1	yes/1	yes/1	yes/1	yes/1		
OTHER INT. IMPROVEMENTS	none	none	none	none	none	none	none	none		
TYPICAL HOUSE VALUE	$325,000	$325,000	$325,000	$325,000	$325,000	$325,000	$325,000	$325,000		
VARIABLE FEATURES	—	poor location	—	year old sale	frame siding	extra half-base	excellent location	no central air		
ADJUSTMENT VALUE OF VARIABLE		$7,000		$5,000	$7,000	$3,000	$10,900	$2,200		

Value Opinion

Using the adjusted values compiled in Figure 7.5, the appraiser can determine the appropriate opinion of market value to assign to the subject property using the sales comparison approach.

Even when the appraiser is dealing with comparable properties that are virtually identical, however, the adjusted values will rarely be identical. Usually, at least some differences in real estate transactions, however minor, will cause selling prices to vary. Whatever the reasons, the adjusted values of the comparable properties will probably not be identical.

No formula exists for reconciling the indicated values. Rather, this involves the application of careful analysis and judgment for which no mathematical formula can be substituted. The appraiser's task is to choose the adjusted value that seems to best reflect the characteristics of the subject property. In other words, which comparable is most like the subject property? The adjusted value of that property will most likely represent the market value of the subject property.

In the sample appraisal, the indicated value of the subject property is $314,000. Here is how the appraiser arrived at that conclusion.

First, the extreme was rejected—Sale 4—because of the large number of adjustments needed. Next, the top seven comparables were ranked, which, in the appraiser's opinion, were most similar to the subject property:

Sale No.	Sales Price	Net Adjustments	Adjusted Sales Price
5	$314,000	0	$314,000
3	311,500	+$ 2,200	313,700
6	319,000	− 3,200	315,800
2	324,400	−10,000	314,400
7	309,000	+ 8,600	317,600
1	310,000	+ 7,130	317,130
8	309,000	+10,800	319,800

Because the value range is close, and because Sale 5 with no adjustments topped the list, the appraiser felt that it was reasonable to assume that the subject property had a market value equal to the adjusted sales price of Sale 5.

APPRAISAL WORKSHEET

1. Using the blank data forms on pages 122–124, describe the neighborhood, site, and house.

2. Find three or four recent sales of houses comparable to the subject property and conduct a comparison analysis. Use the blank Comparable Sales Chart on page 125.

3. Based on your analysis, what is your best opinion of the market value range of the house?_____

NEIGHBORHOOD DATA FORM

BOUNDARIES: ADJACENT TO:

    NORTH _____

    SOUTH _____

    EAST _____

    WEST _____

TOPOGRAPHY: _____ □ URBAN □ SUBURBAN □ RURAL

STAGE OF LIFE CYCLE OF NEIGHBORHOOD:

□ GROWTH □ EQUILIBRIUM □ DECLINE □ REVITALIZATION

% BUILT UP: ____ GROWTH RATE: □ RAPID   □ SLOW   □ STEADY

AVERAGE MARKETING TIME: ____ PROPERTY VALUES: □ INCREASING □ DECREASING □ STABLE

SUPPLY/DEMAND: □ OVERSUPPLY   □ UNDERSUPPLY   □ BALANCED

CHANGE IN PRESENT LAND USE: _____

POPULATION: □ INCREASING □ DECREASING □ STABLE   AVERAGE FAMILY SIZE: _____

AVERAGE FAMILY INCOME _____ INCOME LEVEL: □ INCREASING   □ DECREASING

TYPICAL PROPERTIES:	% OF	AGE	PRICE RANGE	% OWNER OCCUPIED	% RENTALS
VACANT LOTS					
SINGLE-FAMILY RESIDENCES					
2–6-UNIT APARTMENTS					
OVER 6-UNIT APARTMENTS					
NONRESIDENTIAL PROPERTIES					

TAX RATE: _____ □ HIGHER   □ LOWER   □ SAME AS COMPETING AREAS

SPECIAL ASSESSMENTS OUTSTANDING: _____ EXPECTED: _____

SERVICES: □ POLICE   □ FIRE   □ GARBAGE COLLECTION   OTHER: _____

DISTANCE AND DIRECTION FROM

    BUSINESS AREA: _____

    COMMERCIAL AREA: _____

    PUBLIC ELEMENTARY AND HIGH SCHOOLS: _____

    PRIVATE ELEMENTARY AND HIGH SCHOOLS: _____

    RECREATIONAL AND CULTURAL AREAS: _____

    EXPRESSWAY INTERCHANGE: _____

    PUBLIC TRANSPORTATION: _____

       TIME TO REACH BUSINESS AREA: _____COMMERCIAL AREA: _____

    EMERGENCY MEDICAL SERVICE: _____

GENERAL TRAFFIC CONDITIONS: _____

PROXIMITY TO HAZARDS (AIRPORT, CHEMICAL STORAGE, ETC.):_____

PROXIMITY TO NUISANCES (SMOKE, NOISE, ETC.):_____

SITE DATA FORM

ADDRESS: _____

LEGAL DESCRIPTION: _____

_____

_____

_____

_____

_____

DIMENSIONS: _____

SHAPE: _____ SQUARE FEET: _____

TOPOGRAPHY: _____ VIEW: _____

NATURAL HAZARDS: _____

☐ INSIDE LOT   ☐ CORNER LOT   ☐ FRONTAGE _____

ZONING: _____ ADJACENT AREAS: _____

UTILITIES: ☐ ELECTRICITY   ☐ GAS   ☐ WATER   ☐ TELEPHONE
              ☐ SANITARY SEWER   ☐ STROM SEWER

IMPROVEMENTS: DRIVEWAY: _____   STREET: _____
               SIDEWALK: _____   CURB/GUTTER: _____   ALLEY: _____
               STREETLIGHTS: _____

LANDSCAPING: _____

TOPSOIL: _____ DRAINAGE: _____

EASEMENTS: _____

DEED RESTRICTION: _____

SITE PLAT:

BUILDING DATA FORM

ADDRESS: _____

NO. OF UNITS: _____ NO. OF STORIES: _____ ORIENTATION: N S E W

TYPE: _____ DESIGN: _____ AGE: _____ SQUARE FEET: _____

	GOOD	FAIR	POOR
GENERAL CONDITION OF EXTERIOR			
FOUNDATION TYPE _____ BSMT./CRAWL SP./SLAB			
EXTERIOR WALLS: BRICK/BLOCK/VENEER/STUCCO/			
WOOD/COMPOSITE/ALUMINUM/VINYL			
WINDOW FRAMES: METAL/WOOD			
STORM WINDOWS: _____ SCREENS: ____			
GARAGE: _____ ATTACHED/DETACHED			
NUMBER OF CARS: _____			
☐ PORCH ☐ DECK ☐ PATIO ☐ SHED			
OTHER: _____			
GENERAL CONDITION OF INTERIOR			
INTERIOR WALLS: DRYWALL/PLASTER/WOOD			
CEILINGS: _____			
FLOORS: WOOD/CONCRETE/TILE/CARPET			
ELECTRICAL WIRING AND SERVICE: _____			
HEATING PLANT: _____ AGE: _____			
GAS/WOOD/ELECTRIC/SOLAR			
CENTRAL AIR-CONDITIONING: _____ AIR FILTRATION: ___			
NO OF FIREPLACES: _____ TYPE: _____			
OTHER _____			
BATHROOM: FLOOR___WALLS_____FIXTURES _____			
BATHROOM: FLOOR___WALLS_____FIXTURES _____			
BATHROOM: FLOOR___WALLS_____FIXTURES _____			
KITCHEN: FLOOR___WALLS_____CABINETS _____			
FIXTURES _____			

ROOM SIZES	LIVING ROOM	DINING ROOM	KITCHEN	BEDROOM	BATH	CLOSETS	FAMILY ROOM
BASEMENT							
1ST FLOOR							
2ND FLOOR							
ATTIC							

DEPRECIATION (DESCRIBE):

PHYSICAL DETERIORATION _____

FUNCTIONAL OBSOLESCENCE _____

EXTERNAL OBSOLESCENCE_____

COMPARABLE SALES CHART

	SUBJECT	COMPARABLE NO. 1		COMPARABLE NO. 2		COMPARABLE NO. 3		COMPARABLE NO. 4		COMPARABLE NO. 5	
Address											
Proximate to Subject											
Sales Price											
Data Source											
VALUE ADJUSTMENTS	Description	Description	+(-)$ Adjustment	Description	+(-)$ Adjustment	Description	+(-)$ Adjustment	Description	+(-)$ Adjustment	Description	+(-)$ Adjustment
Sales or Financing Concessions		none		none		none					
	Adjusted	$		$		$		$		$	
	Value										
Date of Sale/Time	Adjusted	$		$		$		$		$	
	Value										
Location											
Site/View											
Design and Appeal											
Quality of Construction											
Age											
Condition											
Above Grade	Total Bdrms Baths	Total Bdrms Baths		Total Bdrms Baths		Total Bdrms Baths		Total Bdrms Baths		Total Bdrms Baths	
Room Count											
Gross Living Area	sq. ft.	sq. ft.		sq. ft.		sq. ft.		sq. ft.		sq. ft.	
Basement & Finished											
Room Below Grade											
Functional Utility											
Heating/Cooling											
Garage/Carport											
Other Ext.											
Improvements											
Special Energy											
Efficient Items											
Fireplace(s)											
Other Int.											
Improvements											
Add'l Adj.		□+ □-		□+ □-		□+ □-		□+ □-		□+ □-	
Adjusted											
Value											

Site Valuation

8

Much of the information discussed in this chapter should already be familiar to you, although you may not have thought about it in exactly the way that it is discussed here. To illustrate, let's start with an example.

Example

A three-bedroom, two-bathroom house with an attached two-car garage is constructed on a suburban building lot in Twelve Oaks, Anystate. At the same time, an exact duplicate of the house is constructed by the same builder on a lot of the same size and topography in the neighboring town of Three Maples. The same kinds of materials are used, the same crafts-people are hired to perform the work, and both houses are fitted with the same brand of appliances. Yet the asking price for the house in Twelve Oaks is $285,000, and the asking price for the house in Three Maples is $260,000. Why is there a price differential? In this case, the answer lies in the value of the two parcels of land on which the houses were built. The lot in Twelve Oaks cost the builder $80,000, while the lot in Three Maples cost the builder only $55,000.

There are two basic facts that affect all real estate appraisals:

1. Land value is the primary determinant of overall real estate value.
2. Land value is determined by market demand.

The most luxurious building constructed with the finest materials and the greatest attention to detail, regardless of its construction cost, will be only as valuable as the demand for that kind of property *in that location* warrants. As explained in the first few chapters of this book, market demand is a reflection of the number of possible buyers competing for the available products and services. The number of buyers and sellers in the marketplace for real estate is subject to many variables, including the same factors that affect the country's overall economy, such as income and employment levels. The real estate appraiser's job is to identify the market variables that affect land value as well as possible and to determine their impact on value.

This chapter discusses the basic principles and techniques that enable an appraiser to form an opinion of the market value of land after identifying, gathering, and analyzing the necessary data.

SEPARATE SITE VALUATIONS

Although vacant land can be appraised, most land valuations consider the property's value as a building site. A site is land that has been prepared for its intended use by the addition of such improvements as grading, utilities, and road access. These improvements do not include structures, even though the same term can be used to apply to both. A site, then, is land that is ready for building or that already has a building on it but is being valued separately from the building.

Cost Approach

One of the primary reasons for a separate site valuation is to use the cost approach to value. The cost approach is based on the following formula:

Reproduction or Replacement Cost of Improvement(s)
  − Accrued Depreciation + Site Value = Property Value

Even though the elements of site preparation, such as access and utilities, are improvements to the land, in the cost approach formula the term *improvements* refers to structures. An appraiser using the cost approach will calculate the value of the land separately and then add that value to the depreciated construction cost of the structures. The cost approach is covered in detail in Chapter 9.

Assessments and Taxation

Local communities frequently assess individual property owners for the cost of installation or upkeep of utilities and roads that benefit their property. The amount of the individual assessment is typically based on the value of the site, exclusive of any structures.

Real property taxes are generally ad valorem taxes; that is, they are based on a percentage of property value. Most states require separate valuations of site and structures when determining the property value base to which the property tax rate will be applied.

Structures owned for investment purposes can be depreciated. Their value can be deducted from income produced by the investment over the term allowed by the applicable federal income tax law provision. Because land is *not* considered a wasting asset, its value must be subtracted from the overall property value before the amount of the allowable deduction can be calculated.

Income Capitalization

Using the income capitalization approach to appraising, the appraiser must determine the present value of the right to receive the income stream estimated to be produced by the property that is the subject of the appraisal. One of the methods that relies on income data to determine value is the **building residual technique,** which requires the appraiser to find land value separately. The appraiser subtracts an appropriate return on land value from the net income produced by the property to indicate the income available to the building.

Highest and Best Use

A highest and best use study can be a very complex process. If the appraiser is asked to consider the entire range of uses to which the property could be put, the appraiser must consider the value of the land separately from the value of any particular structure that can be erected on it. The property will be valued both with and without structures. The appraiser will consider not only the most valuable present and prospective use of the site, but also whether a zoning change or other approval necessary for a particular use is likely.

Condemnation Appraisals

When land is condemned for a public or quasi-public purpose, courts will frequently require separate site and building valuations as part of the determination of the property's fair market value.

SITE DATA

The appraiser performing a site appraisal must determine and then collect the necessary data.

Identification

The first step in site analysis is to identify the property. If you have ever heard one of the horror stories about a house built on the wrong subdivision lot, you know the importance of identifying the correct parcel and how easily an error can be made. The appraiser should have a complete and accurate legal description of the entire parcel, as well as its street address, if any. The appraisal report should include maps showing the property's boundaries as well as its location in the neighborhood.

The three major methods of legal description of land used in the United States are the metes and bounds system, the rectangular survey system, and the lot and block system.

Metes and Bounds System

One of the oldest methods of legal description is the **metes and bounds system.** A parcel of land is described by reference to measured distances, called metes, from a stated point of beginning to monuments or markers. Individual markers can be either natural (a large rock or tree) or man-made (a fence post). Figure 8.1 is an example of an early metes and bounds legal description.

Because markers were often removed or destroyed, the need for a more accurate and reliable method of legal description soon became apparent. In many areas, points of beginning have been replaced by permanent markers, and the laser transits used by modern surveyors give extremely accurate results.

Rectangular Survey System

In 1785, Congress established the government survey system, also called the **rectangular survey system** and section and township system. Land area is divided into townships and measured and numbered starting at the intersection of a

Figure 8.1 Metes and Bounds Tract

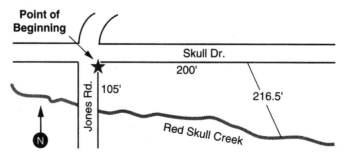

baseline running east to west and a principal meridian running north to south, as shown in Figure 8.2. Lines running east and west, parallel to the baseline and spaced six miles apart, are called township lines. Lines that run north and south, parallel to the principal meridian, are also six miles apart and are called range lines, as shown in Figure 8.3. When the horizontal township lines and the vertical range lines intersect, they form squares that are called sections. A township is divided into 36 sections. A section of land contains 640 acres and is 1 mile square, or 5,280 feet by 5,280 feet.

Sections are numbered 1 through 36, as shown in Figure 8.4. Section 1 is always at the northeast corner of the township, which is the upper right-hand corner if a map of the township is oriented with north at the top. The numbering proceeds right to left, left to right for the next row, right to left for the row after that, and so on. Each section in a township, in turn, can be divided into halves, quarters, and even smaller parcels based on compass point directions, as shown in the example in Figure 8.5.

The area of a fractional part of a section is found by multiplying the fraction (or fractions) by the number of acres in a section—640. The rectangular survey system description of the 40-acre parcel, labeled A in Figure 8.5, is "the NE 1/4 of the SW 1/4 of Section 12."

The appraiser should be familiar with all three forms of legal descriptions and know which forms are accepted in the area where the appraisal is being conducted. This information can be found in Figure 8.6.

Rectangular survey system descriptions are most often used to describe large tracts of land and rural property.

Lot and Block System

Today, most urban and suburban real estate can be referred to by a **lot and block system** description. The lot and block numbers refer to a particular tract shown

Figure 8.2 Township Lines

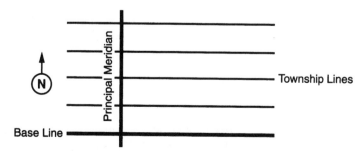

Figure 8.3 Range Lines

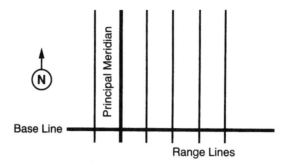

Figure 8.4 Sections in a Township

6	5	4	3	2	1
7	8	9	10	11	12
18	17	16	15	14	13
19	20	21	22	23	24
30	29	28	27	26	25
31	32	33	34	35	36

on a subdivision map on file in the county recorder's office. The description will also identify the city and county in which the tract is located and should provide the book and page number where the subdivision map appears in the county recorder's office, as well as the date the map was recorded.

Figure 8.7 shows part of a subdivision in Riverglen, California. The legal description of lot 7 is the following:

> Lot 7, Fertile Acres, Amended 35/38 (as recorded July 14, 1976, Book 186, Page 19 of maps), City of Riverglen, County of Riverside, State of California.

Analysis

Once the subject property has been identified adequately, it must be analyzed in detail. In addition to general information on economic trends and factors

Figure 8.5 A Section

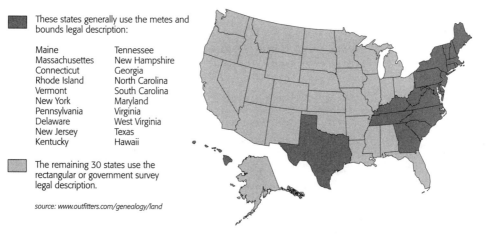

Figure 8.6 Map of United States and Land Description Section

These states generally use the metes and bounds legal description:

Maine	Tennessee
Massachusettes	New Hampshire
Connecticut	Georgia
Rhode Island	North Carolina
Vermont	South Carolina
New York	Maryland
Pennsylvania	Virginia
Delaware	West Virginia
New Jersey	Texas
Kentucky	Hawaii

The remaining 30 states use the rectangular or government survey legal description.

source: www.outfitters.com/genealogy/land

influencing value, the appraiser will need data on property features and other facts, such as the following:

- Size of the site
- Boundaries
- Topography

Figure 8.7 Subdivision Plat Map

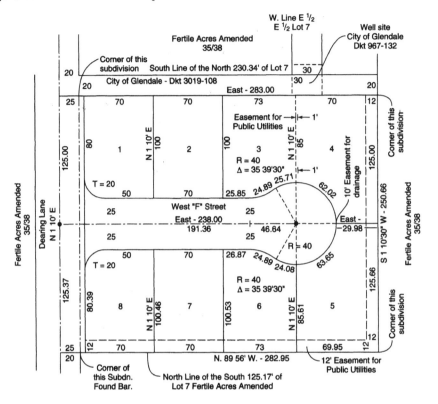

- Location of the site in terms of position on the block
- Utilities and other site improvements
- Soil composition, especially as related to grading, septic system, or bearing capacity for foundations
- Zoning of the subject property and surrounding properties
- Easements, deed restrictions, or publicly held rights-of-way
- Any limitations on the use of the site for building purposes

With all of this information collected and studied, the appraiser is ready to apply one of the site valuation methods discussed in the next section.

METHODS OF SITE VALUATION

Six valuation methods are commonly used when appraising building sites. Two of them, the **land residual method** and ground rent capitalization method, will not be discussed because they are generally used only for commercial properties and require complex calculations of income and lease payments. Following is an explanation of the other four land valuation methods that are used to appraise various kinds of residential real estate.

Sales Comparison Method

Using the **sales comparison method,** sales of similar vacant sites are analyzed and compared. After any necessary adjustments to sales prices are made, the appraiser derives an opinion of value for the subject site. No significant differences exist between the data valuation of improved properties (those with structures) and unimproved sites. Because the sales comparison approach is covered in detail in Chapter 7, it is simply reviewed here.

Of all the methods of site valuation, the sales comparison method generally provides the most reliable indicator of market value. The appraiser's objective is to determine the most probable value of the subject property by interpreting data from sales of similar properties. The appraiser's first task in applying this method is to find sales data on comparable properties. Because no two parcels of land are ever identical, an appraiser will always have to compensate for some differences when comparing sales properties to the subject property. Typical differences include the following:

- Location (block, neighborhood, area)
- Physical characteristics
- Zoning and land-use restrictions
- Terms of financing
- Conditions of sale

Of course, the appraiser is also concerned that the comparable properties have been sold fairly recently. If any sale occurred more than six months before the date of the appraisal, an adjustment is probably indicated.

The adjustment process should eliminate the effect on value of the significant property differences. When adjusting the sales price of a comparable property, lump-sum dollar amounts or percentages are customarily used. Adjustments are always made to the sales price of the comparable property. If the comparable property is inferior in some respect to the subject property, its sales price is increased by an appropriate dollar amount or percentage. If the comparable property is superior in some category to the subject property, its sales price is decreased commensurately.

The appraiser uses the adjusted sales prices to determine the most likely value to assign to the subject property.

Example

A lot in Hilltop Estates is being appraised. Hilltop Estates is a subdivision zoned for single-family residences.

Of the original 110 lots platted, only 7 remain unimproved. The subject property is located at 415 Pamela Court and is 75 by 150 feet with a gentle downhill grade. The most recent lot sales in Hilltop Estates have been those listed as follows:

	Lot A	Lot B	Lot C	Lot D
Address	316 Pamela	506 Aria	384 Paula	717 Rachel
Sales Price	$85,000	$65,000	$75,000	$95,000
Date of Sale	Two months ago	One month ago	Three months ago	Six weeks ago
Financing Concessions	None	None	None	None
Location	Same block as subject	Three blocks from subject	One block from subject	Six blocks from subject
Size	75′ × 140′	75′ × 150′	70′ × 160′	100′ × 145′
Area	10,050 sf	11,250 sf	11,200 sf	14,500 sf
Topography	Downhill	Steep uphill	Flat	Downhill
View	City	Street	Street	City
Utilities	Elect/Gas/ Phone/Cable	Elect/Gas/ Phone/Cable	Elect/Gas/ Phone/Cable	Elect/Gas/ Phone/Cable
Zoning	SF-1	SF-1	SF-1	SF-1
Other	Graded	Not graded	Graded	Graded

The appraiser makes the following adjustments to the sales prices of the comparables:

Lot A—Size, +$1,500	Adjusted Value $86,500
Lot B—Topography, +$5,000; View, +$10,000; Grading, +$5,000	Adjusted Value $85,000
Lot C—Topography, −$5,000; View, +$10,000	Adjusted Value $80,000
Lot D—Size, −$15,000	Adjusted Value $80,000

The adjusted values range from $80,000 to $86,500. Overall, however, Lot A is most similar to the subject property. Lot B, an uphill lot, will require substantial excavation to prepare for building. Lot C, while offering the advantage of flat, buildable space, only has a view of the street and neighboring houses. Lot D is very similar to the subject property, though somewhat larger. For these reasons, and because few lots are available in this desirable subdivision, the appraiser determines that $86,500 is the appropriate opinion of market value for the subject property.

In this example, the appraiser felt justified in selecting an adjusted value that was at the high end of the indicated value range. If the market conditions were not favorable and if more competing properties were on the market, the appraiser would have taken those factors into account and probably would have formed a more conservative (lower) opinion.

Allocation Method

Land value may be treated as a percentage or proportion of the total value of an improved property by using the allocation method. Often, a consistent relationship exists between land and building values. For example, an area may tend to have a one-to-four land-to-building value ratio. This means that the building value will be four times the land value. If the total property value is $500,000, $100,000 will be allocated to the land and $400,000 to the building. This phenomenon occurs partly because developers do not want to overimprove a parcel with a building far in excess of what the value of the site warrants. As a rough rule of thumb, such a ratio will serve as a very broad indicator of what buyers in the marketplace are likely to expect.

As demand for buildable land increases, the ratio of land-to-building value tends to narrow as their relative values come closer together. The one-to-four ratio may become one-to-three or even one-to-two. This occurs because the total cost of the land and building will be limited by what buyers in the marketplace are prepared to pay, although the affordability ceiling will tend to rise as demand increases and supply dwindles. During the past several decades, buyers and renters of residential property have earmarked more and more of their incomes for housing.

An obvious failing of the allocation method is that it does not take into account individual property differences. This method should be relied on only when there is a lack of current data on vacant sites that are comparable to the property being appraised. It may also be useful as a broad check of an appraisal by another method.

Abstraction Method

Abstraction or extraction is similar to the allocation method. As shown in Figure 8.8, all improvement costs less depreciation ($129,000) are deducted from the sales price ($178,000), and the remaining value of $49,000 is considered land value.

The abstraction method, though not precise, may be useful in appraising property when there are few sales for comparison.

Subdivision Development Method

The last land valuation method concerns the value of raw (undeveloped) land that is suitable for single-family residential building lots.

Residential development in and around urban areas is a fact of life, and most sites suitable for single-family houses are part of subdivisions that started out as large tracts of undeveloped land. The 160-acre dairy farm that supported one or more families comfortably becomes—seemingly overnight—the center of a whirlwind as bulldozers move in to prepare the land for home building. If the present residents of the area are lucky, the farmhouse remains as a reminder of simpler times. Once the building sites are prepared and construction is ready to begin, the individual lots will be priced as the market will allow. Because the final pricing will depend to a great extent on the way in which the subdivision is platted, how can a fair value for the raw land be determined?

Figure 8.8 Abstraction Method

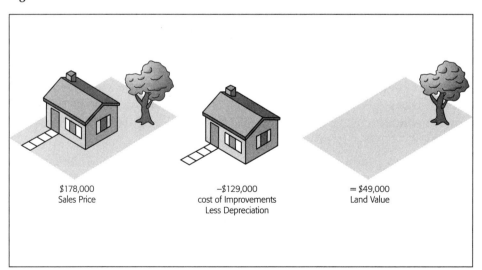

$178,000	−$129,000	= $49,000
Sales Price	cost of Improvements Less Depreciation	Land Value

One method that can be used factors out the expenses of development to determine a fair market value for the land prior to development. In the **subdivision development method**, all probable costs of development, including the developer's profit and cost of financing, are subtracted from the total projected sales prices of the individual units. The figure that results is the value of the raw land.

Example

Happy Hollow Acres is a 40-acre farm that is being considered for subdivision development. Because the land is in the path of a new extension of the interstate highway, its current highest and best use is single-family home development. It is estimated that the property can be divided into 160 buildable lots, after allowing for roads and the open space required by the planning commission. By estimating the probable sales prices of the lots and computing the costs of development, the appraiser can determine the value of the undeveloped land.

Total Projected Sales: 160 lots at $40,000 per lot		$6,400,000
Total Projected Development Costs:		
Street grading and paving, sidewalks, curbs, gutters, sanitary and storm sewers for 160 lots at $12,000 per lot	$1,920,000	
Other costs, including sales office and commissions, estimated at a total of 20% of sales ($6,400,000 × 20%)	1,280,000	
Developer's profit, 10% of projected sales ($6,400,000 × 10%)	640,000	
Total Development Costs		3,840,000
Estimated Value of Raw Land		2,560,000
Raw Land Value per Lot ($2,560,000 ÷ 160)		16,000

This is a very simplified example of the kind of calculations that will take place. Because the eventual site sales would not occur for some time, the appraiser would also have to take into account the time value of the money used to purchase the raw land, whether the developer's or borrowed funds. That is, how much would the developer be willing to pay for the unimproved land, considering the interest that the developer would be losing on the funds that would buy the land, or the interest that the developer would be paying on the loan taken out for the purchase of the land?

In the Happy Hollow Acres example, the total land value was estimated at $2,560,000. It is estimated that the lot sales will take place over three years. The developer expects a yield of 10 percent from the funds invested over those three years *over and above any profit from the work of development.* By applying the appropriate reversion factor to the dollar value of each year's anticipated sales, the *present value* of the undeveloped parcel can be estimated. The calculations are given as follows:

First Year:	60 lots at $16,000 per lot = $960,000	
	$960,000 discounted to present worth at 10 percent for one year (.909)	$872,640
Second Year:	70 lots at $16,000 per lot = $1,120,000	
	$1,120,000 discounted to present worth at 10 percent for two years (.826)	925,120
Third Year:	30 lots at $16,000 per lot = $480,000	
	$480,000 discounted to present worth for three years (.751)	360,480
Present value of $2,560,000 discounted partially over one, two, and three years		$2,158,240
Present discounted lot value		$ 13,489

Based on the projected costs and sales figures for this developer, the present worth of the 40 undeveloped acres is $2,158,240. Note that after taking into account the carrying charges on the development funds invested in the project, the present value of the land required for a single lot decreased from $16,000 to approximately $13,500. Again, this example is greatly simplified. The projected sales prices, for example, will probably be expected to increase over the three years that the lots are sold, which would increase the value per lot. The value of any salvageable structures already on the property would also have to be included.

APPRAISAL WORKSHEET

1. Is the home located in a subdivision?_____

2. If so, how many lots were part of the original subdivision plan?_____

3. How many undeveloped lots are in the subdivision or the immediate vicinity (say, one mile)?_____

4. List three or four recent sales of building lots comparable to the subject and describe each property.

	Lot A	Lot B	Lot C	Lot D
Address				
Sales Price				
Date of Sale				
Financing Concessions				
Location				
Size				
Area				
Topography				
View				
Utilities				
Zoning				
Other				

The Cost Approach

9

One approach to appraising that is especially appropriate for certain types of property is the **cost approach.** To reach an opinion of value by the cost approach, the appraiser (1) calculates the cost to reproduce or replace the existing structures; (2) subtracts from the cost estimate any loss in value because of depreciation; and (3) adds the value of the site alone to the depreciated cost figure.

Following is the formula for the cost approach:

> Reproduction or Replacement Cost of Improvement(s)
> − Accrued Depreciation
> + Site Value
> = Property Value

The value of the land must be figured separately and then added to the depreciated construction cost of the structures. Site value is typically computed by the sales comparison approach, which was explained in the previous chapter. First, the location and improvements (exclusive of buildings) of the subject site are analyzed. Next, the appraiser finds nearby recently sold properties that are comparable to the subject. Adjustments are then made to the sales price of each of those properties to account for any significant differences between the comparable and the subject. Finally, the appraiser forms an opinion of the site value based on the adjusted values of the comparables.

Because the cost approach involves the addition of separately derived building and land values, it is also called the **summation method** of appraising.

THE THEORY BEHIND THE COST APPROACH

The basic premise of the cost approach is this: Under normal market conditions, buyers of real estate typically do not want to pay more for a parcel with an existing structure than they would have to pay to build an identical structure on a vacant parcel. In the same manner, they would not want to pay as much for an older building as they would pay for a brand-new one. Every used building will have suffered some of the effects of ordinary wear and tear and may not be of the currently most desirable design or contain the most up-to-date fixtures. As a result, an older building should not be as expensive as a brand-new building of the same size that offers the features that are currently in the greatest demand.

There are exceptions to every rule, of course, and you may have already thought of several exceptions to the application of the cost approach to appraising real estate. Some properties are more valuable *because* of their age and are priced accordingly. Most urban areas have a historic district in which the historical landmark designation can be either a blessing or a bane. It can be a blessing if it means that property will retain its character and charm for the enjoyment of all who live in the community. It can be a bane for the property owner if considerable effort and financial commitment are required to bring the property to livable standards within the limitations typically placed on historic properties. Fortunately, our tax laws offer incentives to those who choose to invest in rehabilitating historic structures. Partly because of that advantage, habitable buildings with historic status tend to be more valuable than similar buildings without such a designation.

The realities of the marketplace may also appear to make a mockery of the cost approach. Most regions of the United States, at one time or another, have experienced the red-hot seller's market—the kind of market in which the typical property elicits multiple bids soon after being offered for sale. When an overabundance of buyers confronts a market with relatively few properties for sale, prices tend to rise at sometimes incomprehensible rates. Often, the cost of a used house rises to meet or even surpass that of a new house that may be less accessible or may not be immediately available for occupancy. Most areas of the country have experienced the effects of a real estate boom at one time or another. Property owners in recent times can attest to the marvelous ease with which property can be sold in the seller's market that accompanies a real estate boom.

Unfortunately for sellers, but fortunately for buyers, most markets tend to cool off eventually. Sometimes the cooling off is so precipitous that the boom turns into a bust and produces the opposite effect—the buyer's market. Many homeowners who gleefully anticipated their potential profits during the hot days of a seller's market know the cold feeling of desperation that comes from having to sell a house that no one is interested in buying. Even worse, some of those buyers who purchased when prices were at all-time highs are forced to sell their properties at a loss, the ultimate market dilemma that most of us don't like to think of in relation to one of our most valuable financial assets—our home.

APPLYING THE COST APPROACH FORMULA

Several other, more technical drawbacks to the application of the cost approach exist, particularly when it is applied to residential property.

First, the existing property use may not be the land's highest and best use. If the structure being appraised is inappropriate and not easily adaptable to the site's highest and best use, a cost approach analysis may be an idle exercise. One example that occurs frequently in urban areas is the residential neighborhood that is rezoned to allow commercial development. As properties in the area are converted to commercial use, their land value typically increases. The value of any structures may increase as well, but the structures with the greatest increase in value will be those that are adaptable for business use.

Second, builders' costs always vary to some extent depending on the number of projects undertaken and the individual builder's profit margin, among other factors. The real estate appraiser's job is to be aware of the range of construction costs in the area in order to select the figure that is most appropriate for the property being appraised.

REPRODUCTION COST VERSUS REPLACEMENT COST

The appraiser always begins the cost approach valuation by estimating the construction cost of a new building that is physically or functionally identical to the building that is the subject of the appraisal, *at current prices*. The physical condition of the building and the outside factors that may affect its value are not considered at this stage. The construction cost computed by the appraiser will be either the reproduction cost or the replacement cost of the subject. Although the terms *reproduction cost* and *replacement cost* may appear synonymous, they have very different meanings in a real estate appraisal.

Reproduction Cost

Reproduction cost is the dollar amount required to produce an exact duplicate of a building at current prices. The appraiser must take into account the expense of finding materials of the same design, manufacture, and quality as the subject property, constructed with the same techniques.

For properties that are of relatively recent origin, this is usually a feasible task that results in a cost analysis in keeping with other structures of current vintage. For older buildings, however, particularly those that have attained historic status, the task of estimating the current reproduction cost becomes considerably more formidable. The appraiser is confronted with materials that may no longer be available or that may be impossible to duplicate except at an exorbitant cost. In addition, certain property features requiring sophisticated carpentry, masonry, or other skills may be beyond the expertise of today's craftspeople.

Because most existing structures are fairly recent in origin, finding the reproduction cost is usually not a problem and is how appraisers use the cost approach. For properties that do not have an economically viable reproduction cost, the appraiser will calculate the replacement cost of the structures instead.

Replacement Cost

Replacement cost is the current construction cost of a building with the same utility as the subject structure. The appraiser is actually estimating the reproduction cost, but it is the reproduction cost of a theoretical building that contains the same number, type, and size of rooms as the building being appraised and that can be used in the same way. The appraiser does not take into account the many details of material and workmanship that may make the subject property unique. The theoretical building against which the subject is measured should possess the same overall quality as the subject, but as defined by contemporary standards.

Of course, the appraiser will note as a condition of the appraisal that it is impossible to duplicate the subject property exactly in today's marketplace. The appraiser will also have to gauge the effect of this condition on the property's value. The existing property features may be more or less valuable, depending on the desirability of those features in the marketplace.

For example, an older home may have intricate exterior and interior carpentry well beyond the type of work available today. In such a case, the appraiser will estimate the cost to produce features of a similar quality, using currently available construction materials and methods. Many architectural details, such as elaborate moldings (ceiling trim), can be found in materials that look identical to the originals from which they are copied. Yet because the copies are formed from lightweight, synthetic materials, they are relatively inexpensive and easy to install. Figure 9.1 shows some of the types of trim pieces for exterior or interior use that can be formed from polyurethane.

Figure 9.1 Ornamental Finishing Materials

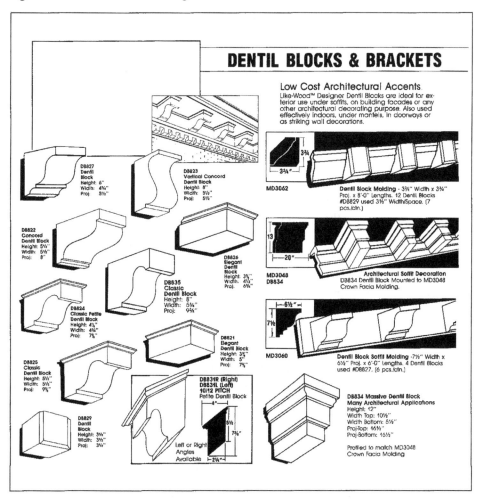

Source: Like-wood™, 2550 Boyce Plaza Road, Pittsburgh, PA 15241

FINDING THE REPRODUCTION COST

Four basic methods can be used to find the building reproduction cost. The most complex are used primarily for commercial and industrial properties. The first method described—the square foot method—is the one that is used most often when appraising single-family residences. The other methods of computing construction cost are described to give you some idea of how other structures are appraised.

Methods Used

1. *Square foot method.* With the **square foot method,** the current construction cost per square foot of the type of building being appraised is multiplied by the number of square feet in the subject building. For example, the current cost per square foot of a single-story house in the Rolling Hills area is about $125. Because the house being appraised is 2,100 square feet, its estimated construction cost at today's prices can be computed as follows:

$$2{,}100 \times \$125 = \$262{,}500$$

In this example, the current estimated construction cost of the house being appraised is $262,500.

2. *Unit-in-place method.* Using the **unit-in-place method,** the appraiser computes the construction cost per unit of measure (usually price per square foot) of each component part of the subject building, including the dollar amounts necessary for material, labor, overhead, and builder's profit. The cost per unit of measure is then multiplied by the number of units of that component part in the subject building. In some cases, the unit is a single element, such as a plumbing fixture, rather than a measure of area. For example, one of the component parts of the building will be the foundation. The appraiser will measure the cost per measured unit of the type of foundation required. For example, the foundation of a storage facility consists of a 12-inch concrete wall and footings covering a building that is 100 by 125 feet. The current cost to build such a foundation is $30.70 per linear foot. The appraiser estimates the number of linear feet in the foundation, then computes the construction cost of that component:

$$100' + 100' + 125' + 125' = 450 \text{ linear feet}$$
$$450 \times \$30.70 = \$13{,}815$$

The current cost of the foundation is $13,815. This amount will be added to the cost of each of the other building components, such as floor, framing, roof construction, windows, doors, heating, air-conditioning, and plumbing fixtures to derive the total current construction cost of the building being appraised.

3. *Quantity survey method.* In the **quantity survey method,** direct and indirect construction costs are itemized separately, then totaled. Direct construction costs are those related to materials and labor, such as clearing the land, laying the foundation, lumber and carpentry, drywall, insulation, cabinetry,

electrical wiring, plumbing, and fixtures. Indirect costs include such expenses as the building permit, overhead, payroll taxes, and builder's profit. For example, an eight-unit apartment building could be constructed today at a cost of $930,383 for all materials and labor. Indirect construction costs, including the building permit, survey, layout, payroll taxes, insurance, builder's overhead, and profit, would be $125,050. When appraising the building, the direct and indirect costs would be totaled as follows:

$$\$930,383 + \$125,050 = \$1,055,433$$

Thus, the building's current construction cost is $1,055,433.

4. *Index method.* With the index method, the appraiser applies a factor representing the change in building costs over time to the original cost of the subject property. For example, consider a building that originally cost $100,000 to build in 1985. The cost index factor for 1985 is 100, while the cost index factor for the present year is 378. The current construction cost of the subject building can be computed as follows:

$$\$100,000 \times 378/100 =$$
$$\$100,000 \times 3.78 =$$
$$\$378,000$$

In this example, the current estimated reproduction cost of the subject structure is $378,000. Because this method of estimating reproduction cost fails to take into account the many variables that can affect construction costs, it never should be used as the sole method of determining the construction cost but only as a quick means of double-checking the estimate reached by one of the other methods.

Applying the Square Foot Method

With experience, the appraiser can become as familiar with local building costs as a contractor is. One of the ways in which both building and appraisal professionals keep up to date on current costs is by using a cost manual. Information on building specifications and typical construction costs is provided in manuals published by such national companies as F. W. Dodge Corporation (*www.fwdodge.com*), Marshall & Swift (*www.marshallswift.com*), and R.S. Means (*www.rsmeans.com*). Cost manuals are customized for specific geographic regions and are usually updated at least annually and sometimes even monthly. A page from a typical residential cost manual appears in Figure 9.2.

Figure 9.2 Typical Page from a Residential Cost Manual

Average 2 Story		MAN-HOURS	COST PER SQUARE FOOT OF LIVING AREA		
Living Area 2000 S.F. / Perimeter 135 L.F.			MAT.	LABOR	TOTAL
1 Site Work	Site preparation for slab; trench 4' deep for foundation wall.	.034		.67	.67
2 Foundations	Continuous concrete footing 8" deep x 18" wide; cast-in-place concrete wall, 8" thick, 4' deep, 4" concrete slab on 4" crushed stone base, trowel finish.	.066	1.77	1.87	3.64
3 Framing	2" x 4" wood studs, 16" O.C.; 1/2" plywood sheathing; 2" x 6" rafters 16" O.C. with 1/2" plywood sheathing; 4 in 12 pitch; 2" x 6" ceiling joists 16" O.C.; 2" x 8" floor joists 16" O.C. with bridging and 5/8" waferboard subfloor; 1/2" waferboard subfloor on 1" x 2" wood sleepers 16" O.C.	.131	3.62	4.15	7.77
4 Exterior Walls	Horizontal beveled wood siding; #15 felt building paper; 3-1/2" batt insulation; wood double hung windows; 3 flush solid core wood exterior doors; storms and screens.	.111	8.71	3.76	12.47
5 Roofing	240# asphalt shingles; #15 felt building paper; aluminum flashing; 6" attic insulation. Aluminum gutters and downspouts.	.024	.39	.59	.98
6 Interiors	1/2" drywall, taped and finished, painted with primer and 1 coat; softwood baseboard and trim, painted with primer and 1 coat; finished hardwood floor 40%, carpet with underlayment 40%, vinyl tile with underlayment 15%, ceramic tile with underlayment 5%; hollow core doors.	.232	9.28	7.90	17.18
7 Specialties	Kitchen cabinets - 14 L.F. wall and base cabinets with laminated plastic counter top; medicine cabinet, stairs.	.021	.93	.33	1.26
8 Mechanical	1 lavatory, white, wall hung; 1 water closet, white; 1 bathtub with shower, porcelain enamel steel, white; 1 kitchen sink, stainless steel, single; 1 water heater, gas fired, 30 gal.; gas fired forced air heat.	.060	1.57	1.34	2.91
9 Electrical	200 Amp. service; romex wiring; incandescent lighting fixtures, switches, receptacles.	.039	.50	.80	1.30
10 Overhead	Contractor's overhead and profit.		1.87	1.50	3.37
Total			28.64	22.91	51.55

The overall quality of construction and type of structure are specified (in this case, the structure is an average-quality, two-story house having a living area of 2,000 square feet and a perimeter of 135 linear feet). The building is first categorized by the quality of its construction, in ascending order: economy, average, custom, or luxury. Next, the typical cost per square foot is broken down into basic building components, from site work to overhead. In this way, the cost estimate for the subject property can be further individualized.

In addition to this very broad itemization of building costs, the manual also lists separate construction features, such as window systems, in a separate section in greater detail and gives cost figures for both materials and labor. Finally, tables provide multiplication factors that take into account the regional variances in material, labor, and other costs. For example, a factor of 1.21 for San Francisco, California, indicates that a home in San Francisco will typically cost 21 percent more than the standard used in the manual.

Most libraries will provide copies of construction cost manuals. Many newspapers also publish periodic listings of average home construction costs in the area.

Example

Josephine and Martin Smith own a two-story home in Leafy Meadow, North Carolina. The house, which is 15 years old, is of average-quality construction for the area and has a total of 2,000 square feet. A current cost manual available at the public library suggests that typical construction costs for a two-story home of the same quality and with the same features are $75 per square foot. The manual also lists a regional factor of .85 for Leafy Meadow, North Carolina. This differential takes into account the relatively low costs of labor and certain materials in Leafy Meadow. The total cost and regional influence can be computed as follows:

$$2,000 \times \$75 = \$150,000$$
$$\$150,000 \times .85 = \$127,500$$

Using the cost manual information, the current cost to build the Smith house is estimated at $127,500.

ACCRUED DEPRECIATION

Depreciation is the kind of term that everyone can define, yet few people can apply. **Depreciation** is a loss in value from *any* cause.

Accrued depreciation is the total loss in value from all causes as of the date of the appraisal. There are three basic forms of depreciation:

1. **Physical deterioration** is the actual destruction of a building, whether from natural or man-made forces. Physical deterioration can occur gradually, as when a building undergoes ordinary wear and tear. It can also happen quickly, for example, when a building is damaged by occupants (rock through a window) or by natural forces (a storm or earthquake).

2. **Functional obsolescence** takes place when a building's layout, design, or other features are considered undesirable in comparison with features designed for the same functions in newer properties. In new homes with two or more bedrooms, one bedroom is typically designated as the master bedroom and is sized accordingly. If the home has three or more bedrooms, it will almost always have more than one bathroom, and one of the bathrooms will adjoin the master bedroom. The three-bedroom home that does not have a master suite or which has only one bathroom may be functionally obsolete, depending on what buyers in the area expect.

3. **External obsolescence** is loss in value from any cause outside the subject property. External obsolescence is also called **environmental, economic,** or **locational obsolescence.** These synonyms give you some idea of the range of the outside factors that can lower property values. The most conspicuous source of external obsolescence these days may be the environmental hazard. Proximity to a known hazard, even when the subject property can be scientifically demonstrated to be unaffected directly by the hazard, will tend to lower property value.

Some form of depreciation, at least physical deterioration, begins the moment a building is completed. The building will suffer some type of depreciation during its entire **economic life,** the period during which it can be used for its originally intended purpose. A building's economic life is also called its **useful life.** Economic life is not necessarily the length of time that the building is expected to remain standing, which is its **physical life.** Of course, not all buildings deteriorate as rapidly as others, and some will benefit from better upkeep. If a building has received regular maintenance and repair, its **effective age** (apparent age) may be less than its actual age.

For appraisal purposes, the most important time measure is the building's **remaining economic life.** This is the period from the date of the appraisal during which the building can be expected to remain useful for its original purpose.

Although the definition of depreciation is simple enough, it can be confusing to understand and difficult to compute. One source of confusion stems from the fact that the property may be also depreciated for tax purposes. Depreciation for tax purposes has no relationship to the depreciation that an appraiser will measure to determine property value. Tax depreciation is a means of writing off (deducting from income) the cost of a building over whatever term of years is permitted by law. Because the federal government recognizes that a building is a deteriorating asset, it allows the cost of the building to be balanced against income produced by it, in yearly increments. The term over which the depreciation is taken, however, has no relationship to either the age or the condition of the property. In fact, both the term of years and the rate of depreciation per year are factors the Internal Revenue Service (IRS) changes often at the will of Congress.

The computations for tax depreciation are involved more with the impact of the allowed deduction on current tax income than with the extent to which the property has deteriorated or otherwise suffered a loss in value. Generally, taxpayers are happier when depreciation deductions are allowed over fewer years (creating a higher deduction per year), and tax collectors are happier when depreciation deductions are spread out over a longer term. Throughout the rest of this chapter and book, therefore, depreciation will refer to a property's actual loss in value and not the arbitrary rate of loss dictated by the tax laws.

Appraisers use several methods to measure depreciation, which are discussed in the following sections.

Age-Life Method

The **age-life method** of computing depreciation is the simplest to understand and use. The building's construction cost is divided by the number of years of its economic life to find a yearly dollar amount of depreciation. The yearly amount of depreciation is then multiplied by the effective age of the building to determine the total amount by which it has depreciated. As a formula, the age-life method is as follows:

$$\frac{\text{Building Cost}}{\text{Number of Years of Economic Life}} \times \text{Effective Age} = \text{Total Accrued Depreciation}$$

Figure 9.3 shows how the relationship between building cost and projected age can be graphed along a straight line. For this reason, the age-life method is also called the **straight-line method** of computing depreciation. The remaining building value at any building age can be found by finding the point on the graphed line where the age factor intersects the cost factor.

In the example plotted in Figure 9.3, the current building cost is $200,000, and the estimated economic life of the building is 50 years. When the building has an economic life of 40 years, its remaining value will be $40,000 because it will have depreciated by $160,000.

Figure 9.3 Age-Life Depreciation

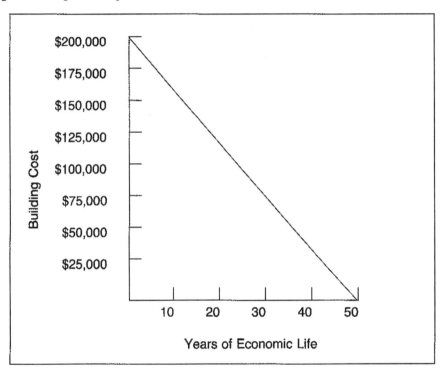

The age-life method of computing depreciation fails to take into account the many variables that can cause a loss in value. For this reason, its use requires that the amount and kinds of depreciation the property has undergone be fairly straightforward (generally, ordinary wear and tear) and also typical of the area. Because most properties will require a more detailed depreciation analysis, another method may have to be used, at least for certain items.

Observed-Condition Method

In the **observed-condition method** of computing depreciation, the appraiser analyzes the property in terms of each of the separate categories of depreciation. The appraiser notes whether each item of depreciation is curable, if it can be easily and economically repaired or replaced, or incurable, if repairs would be cumbersome or too expensive. This method also is called the breakdown method.

Curable physical deterioration includes such repairs as a broken appliance or window and other items of routine maintenance. Examples of **incurable physical deterioration** include those building components that could be repaired or replaced only with great difficulty, such as a foundation that has suffered mudslide damage. Ordinarily, these building components are expected to last for the life of the building. Loss caused by physical deterioration can be valued as a percentage of total building value, or the appraiser can value each depreciated item separately.

Functional obsolescence includes physical or design features that are inadequate or undesirable by current standards. Functional obsolescence can be curable if the existing layout or design can be changed economically. For example, a bedroom next to the kitchen could be converted to a desired family room or den. Most often, however, functional obsolescence is incurable. A typical example is the room layout that could be changed only by expensive remodeling, such as a bedroom that can be entered solely through another bedroom.

Another common example of functional obsolescence is the outdated kitchen. If a property seller is willing to modernize appliances and cabinets, the amount spent remodeling the outdated kitchen may result in an equal increase in value, depending on market demand. The loss in value for appraisal purposes is calculated as the amount by which the entire property value could be increased by making the improvement, rather than the improvement's actual cost to the property owner. In other words, not every dollar spent will result in a corresponding dollar increase in value. This is an important point to remember if a homeowner is considering a remodeling project solely as a means of making the home more salable.

External obsolescence is considered incurable only. Because this form of depreciation is caused by factors outside the property, the owner most likely has no immediate, practical way of remedying it. The interstate highway that creates noise and pollution for nearby residents may be an annoying fact of life, but a fact of life, nonetheless. Don't forget that external obsolescence can be caused by economic factors. The appraiser should be acutely aware of the effect on value of a depressed real estate market. In particular, the appraiser should note the apparent effect of economic conditions on recent sales or rentals of comparable properties.

Market Extraction Method

With the market extraction method of computing depreciation, the appraiser uses the sales prices of comparable properties to derive the value of a depreciated feature. By analyzing enough comparable properties, the appraiser isolates the value of the depreciated feature. This method is also referred to as the market comparison or sales comparison method.

ITEMIZING ACCRUED DEPRECIATION

Total accrued depreciation is calculated by listing each of the categories of depreciation, estimating the loss in value attributable to each of the categories, and totaling the amounts listed.

Example

The Firestone house is being appraised. After conducting a thorough examination of the property, the appraiser estimates the following items of curable physical depreciation:

Item	Reproduction Cost	Percent Depreciation	Amount of Depreciation
Carpeting	$3,500	20%	$700
Air Conditioner Compressor	1,400	70	980
Water Heater	350	100	350

The total reproduction cost of the depreciated items is $3,500 + $1,400 + $350, or $5,250. The total amount of depreciation represented by those items is $700 + $980 + $350, or $2,030.

Because other forms of physical deterioration are generally based on overall wear and tear, the appraiser will determine a percentage of depreciation for all remaining items and apply that percentage *after* subtracting the reproduction cost of the items separately depreciated.

General wear and tear to the Firestone house is estimated at 20 percent of its $200,000 reproduction cost. Depreciation caused by physical deterioration is thus estimated as follows:

$$\$200,000 - \$5,250 = \$194,750$$
$$\$194,750 \times 20\% = \$38,950$$
$$\$38,950 + \$2,030 = \$40,980$$

The appraiser will note $40,980 as a deduction from the construction cost for physical deterioration. The next category of depreciation is functional obsolescence.

The Firestone house has three bedrooms and off the master bedroom is a separate room, which can be entered only from the master bedroom. The extra room serves as a home office and sitting area. This arrangement was actually a building option offered by the developer. Instead of leaving a wall opening in this room for a doorway from the hall, the builder placed the only entrance in a wall shared with the master bedroom. Very few homes in the subdivision utilize this option. Most homes have four bedrooms, all with separate entrances. In this area, prospective buyers typically want four bedrooms and are likely to want to use this space for a bedroom, which means that any other arrangement is awkward and undesirable. The appraiser considers this a form of functional obsolescence. By analyzing sales of other properties in the area with similar features, the appraiser determines that the fact that this fourth "bedroom" does not have a separate entrance indicates that the market value of the house is approximately $3,000 less.

The deduction from the reproduction cost for functional obsolescence is $3,000. The final category of depreciation is external obsolescence.

The Firestone house is located in a quiet residential neighborhood that originally was developed about 20 years ago. The zoning is entirely single-family residential, houses generally have been well maintained, and the close proximity of the area to the suburban business district has resulted in a steady market demand. There are no nearby nuisances and no foreseeable changes to the surrounding land uses. As a result, the appraiser determines that no adjustment is necessary for external obsolescence.

Deductions for depreciation are $40,980 for physical deterioration and $3,000 for functional obsolescence, making the total accrued depreciation $43,980. Land value has already been estimated at $60,000. The appraiser is ready to compute a market value estimate by the cost approach:

Reproduction Cost	$200,000
Less Accrued Depreciation	– 43,980
Subtotal	$156,020
Plus Land Value	60,000
Indicated Market Value	$216,020

The indicated market value of the Firestone house using the cost approach is $216,020.

COST APPROACH USING THE URAR FORM

The cost approach analysis section of the Uniform Residential Appraisal Report (URAR) form, which is shown in Figure 9.4, requires the appraiser to complete the following tasks:

- Develop an opinion of the site value
- Compute the area of the dwelling
- Estimate the reproduction or replacement cost of the dwelling at current market prices
- Compute the area of any garage, carport, or other structure and estimate reproduction cost at current market prices
- Estimate the amount by which the structures have depreciated
- Estimate the "as is" value of any other site improvements, such as landscaping, driveway, fences, and so on, provided they are not included in the Opinion of Site Value line
- Add site value to the depreciated cost of improvements to find the indicated value
- Explain in the comments section how the cost approach was applied and comment on items such as the source of cost data, types of depreciation found, and how the site value was derived

The appraisal will usually include an addendum showing a rough sketch of the perimeter of the subject structure(s), with dimensions given in feet.

USEFULNESS OF THE COST APPROACH

The reproduction cost of a building tends to set the upper limit of its value. There can be, however, a significant difference between the current cost to reproduce a structure and its market value. If the improvements are not new, the appraiser must estimate the amount of accrued depreciation that the property has suffered and deduct that amount from the reproduction cost. For very old buildings, estimating depreciation will be much more difficult. Added to that problem is the fact that today's marketplace may not produce any suitable equivalents to the construction materials and techniques used in an older structure. For those buildings, the sales comparison or income capitalization approach may be most appropriate.

The cost approach is especially useful when valuing buildings for which the sales comparison approach or income capitalization approach is impracticable. Examples include schools, museums, libraries, and other institutional structures.

Figure 9.4 Cost Approach Analysis Section of URAR Form

COST APPROACH TO VALUE (not required by Fannie Mae)				
Provide adequate information for the lender/client to replicate the below cost figures and calculations.				
Support for the opinion of site value (summary of comparable land sales or other methods for estimating site value)				
ESTIMATED ☒ REPRODUCTION OR ☐ REPLACEMENT COST NEW	OPINION OF SITE VALUE			= $ *50,000*
Source of cost data	Dwelling *2,000* Sq. Ft. @ $*95*		....	=$*190,000*
Quality rating from cost service Effective date of cost data	Sq. Ft. @ $		....	=$
Comments on Cost Approach (gross living area calculations, depreciation, etc.)			*Extra (pool)*	*20,000*
See sketch for measurement analysis. Cost estimate	Garage/Carport *625* Sq. Ft. @ $*25*		....	=$ *15,625*
based on current costs of local contractors and	Total Estimate of Cost-New		....	= $ *225,625*
verified by current cost manual. The depreciation	Less Physical	Functional	External	
estimate reflects observed effective age. Site value	Depreciation *36,000*			=$*(36,000)*
supported by market data on comparable sites.	Depreciated Cost of Improvements...			=$ *189,625*
	"As-is" Value of Site Improvements..			=$ *8,000*
Estimated Remaining Economic Life (HUD and VA only) Years	Indicated Value By Cost Approach			=$ *247,625*

Generally, few, if any, comparable sales for such properties will exist, and no income figures will be available.

For certain appraisal purposes, the cost approach may be the *only* feasible approach. In an appraisal for insurance purposes, for instance, insured value will be based on the cost of restoration, which will dictate the amount of reimbursement for loss.

Example: A Tale of Two Houses

The Newsomes and the Palermos own houses on Oak Street in the town of Riverdale, Ohio. Both families purchased their homes when the subdivision was first developed 10 years ago.

The Palermos have maintained their home with meticulous attention. Even the garage, with its shelving designed by Mrs. Palermo and built by Mr. Palermo, is spotless. The Palermos simply enjoy all forms of household chores. They recently devoted a week of vacation time to repainting the exterior of their house in a soft colonial blue.

The Newsomes, on the other hand, hate working around the house almost as much as they hate paying someone else to do so. As a result, their home, though only a block away and of the same age, design, and construction quality as the Palermos' house, has developed some obvious as well as some not so obvious problems.

The exterior and interior of the Newsome house have an overall tired appearance. There are numerous marks on the walls and the rugs. The grease-stained kitchen cabinets and appliances bear the scars of many careless gestures. The mantel above the fireplace has been darkened by smoke. The ceramic tile in the shower stalls is broken in some places and discolored from years of grime, mold, and mildew that has never been adequately removed. In one of the bedrooms, the walls have been severely battered by an overzealous child learning to tap dance. The tile on the laundry floor is buckling because the washing machine discharge hose continually leaks.

The Newsomes' garage door can't be lifted ever since one of the hinges pulled out of the frame when someone accidentally drove into it. The Newsomes don't mind, because they prefer to use their garage for storing their collection of broken appliances rather than for parking. Outside, things aren't any better. The paint on the wood siding is peeling badly. The rain gutters have never been cleaned, and one section of gutter is dangling since it collapsed from the weight of accumulated debris and ice during the past winter. Last, but not least, the shrubbery is unkempt and the lawn has been taken over by weeds.

Pamela Palermo and Frank Newsome work for the same company, which has announced that it is relocating to a smaller city about 325 miles from Riverdale. Pamela and Frank are both invited to make the move. The company will pay for their moving expenses and will reimburse them for their home sale expenses as well, including the brokerage commission. The Palermos and the Newsomes decide to take the company up on its offer. Both families call on the same real estate agent for a market analysis of the sales potential of their homes.

The Palermos are pleased when the agent compliments them on the beautiful appearance of their yard and home. As they relax around the dining room table, the agent tells them that, based on sales of similar properties in the neighborhood, the market value of their home should fall in the range of $225,000 to $240,000. The Palermos then talk with several other agents, who provide a similar value analysis.

Down the street, the Newsomes are anxious to hear what the agent has to say about the value of their home. The agent is very pleasant as she walks around and through the house, even though she trips on the edge of the tile floor in the laundry room and narrowly avoids walking into the dangling gutter. Because the Newsomes know that the Palermos have just listed their property with the same agent for $235,000, they expect that she will suggest a similar figure for their house. They are very surprised, however, when the agent tells them that she strongly recommends that they have a structural pest-control inspection to confirm or eliminate the possibility of termite damage. Apart from any work indicated by the termite report, she believes that the market value of their home is somewhere in the range of $200,000 to $210,000 *if* they clean and paint the entire house, inside and out, replace the laundry room tile floor, clean out the garage, fix the broken garage door, repair the damaged bedroom walls, retile the bathrooms, and repair or replace the gutters. The yard area should be reseeded or at least weeded and the shrubbery pruned. They should also consider refinishing the kitchen cabinets. If they don't accomplish these tasks, their house is probably worth considerably less than $200,000 and, if they're serious about selling, they shouldn't ask more than $185,000 to $190,000 for it to attract a buyer. The agent's explanation refers to such things as "deferred maintenance," "deterioration," and "curb appeal."

The Newsomes, when they recover from their shock, decide to contact a few other agents. Unfortunately, the value opinions don't seem to get any higher. Frank Newsome schedules a meeting with his company's relocation officer to find out whether the company will pay for the necessary maintenance and repairs to his home as expenses of sale. He isn't reassured by the answer he receives, but he decides to go ahead with the job transfer and home sale despite what he calls the "lousy" real estate market.

The Newsomes shouldn't have been surprised at the low valuation of their home in comparison to that of the Palermos. Even though the homes are in the same neighborhood and are comparable in size, design, and quality of construction, the Palermos have maintained their home diligently over the years, while the Newsomes have neglected theirs. The results of these efforts (or lack thereof) show in the general condition and appearance of the two homes.

APPRAISAL WORKSHEET

1. When was the subject house built?_____

2. How old is it now? _____

3. How old are other buildings in the neighborhood? _____

4. What is the cost per square foot of similar new houses? _____

5. Are the materials and construction techniques used to build the subject house in common use today? _____

6. Does the neighborhood have other houses with design and construction features comparable to those of the subject house? _____

7. What unique design or construction features does the house have? _____

8. What design or construction features does the house have that are considered undesirable by today's homebuyers? _____

9. What is the zoning for the neighborhood and is it expected to change in the future?_____

10. Are nearby land uses compatible with the neighborhood? _____

11. What adverse environmental influences are there in the neighborhood and what have been their impact on property values? _____

12. How can economic conditions (the current market) be expected to affect the value of the house? _____
_____

Rate each of the following features of the property as good, fair, or poor:

	Good	Fair	Poor
General exterior condition	____	____	____
Exterior siding	____	____	____
Masonry	____	____	____
Gutters and trim	____	____	____
General interior condition	____	____	____
Floors	____	____	____
Walls and ceilings	____	____	____
Cabinets and wood trim	____	____	____
Bathrooms	____	____	____
Fixtures (heating and a/c unit, water heater, appliances)	____	____	____
Garage condition	____	____	____
Landscaping	____	____	____
Design	____	____	____
Upkeep	____	____	____
Amenities (porch, deck, pool)	____	____	____

The Income Capitalization Approach

10

Although the income capitalization approach has a formidable title, it is based on a relatively simple premise: The value of a property is related to the income it can produce. The more income the property produces, the more the property tends to be worth. An investor will pay more for a property that produces a certain level of income than for a property that produces less income.

The income capitalization approach is most useful, of course, for properties that are purchased strictly for their ability to produce income. These typically include commercial properties, such as office buildings and retail stores. Less often, investors purchase industrial properties, such as manufacturing plants, for their income potential. An investor determines the price to offer for a potential acquisition by studying the income generated by the property and by determining the present value of the right to receive that income in the future, taking into account the rate of income, or capitalization rate, that the investor expects to receive.

The following formula is used for the **income capitalization approach:**

$$\frac{\text{Net Operating Income}}{\text{Capitalization Rate}} = \text{Value}$$

The income capitalization approach is usually the most appropriate appraisal method to use for commercial and industrial properties, which are generally purchased for their income-producing potential. The same can be said of residential property with more than four dwelling units. The buyer of an apartment building will be interested in the cash flow the property generates, that is, the amount of profit that can be expected over and above the expenses of ownership. Smaller multiunit buildings with only two to four apartments can also be purchased primarily for their income-producing potential, but very often they are owner-occupied, and the benefits of living in the building have to be weighed against the loss of income from the owner-occupied unit.

Single-family houses, on the other hand, are not usually purchased for their income-producing potential. Even though many single-family homes are purchased by investors, the vast majority of single-family residences are owner-occupied, and the amount of income they could generate is not a factor in the decision to buy. Still, a variation of the income capitalization approach can be used by anyone who is interested in the income-producing capability of a single-family house. This approach compares the monthly rent paid for similar homes to the sales prices of those homes. This is to derive a factor that can be multiplied by the income expected from the subject property to calculate market value. This simpler version of the income approach, called the **gross rent multiplier (GRM),** was previously discussed in chapter three.

This chapter will cover the types of information required to apply either version of the income capitalization approach, as well as the ways in which the information is derived.

DETERMINING INCOME

Because the income capitalization approach is concerned with the amount of income a piece of real estate produces, important data to be collected by the appraiser using this method will be complete information on the potential gross income the property can generate. The appraiser will take into account both rental income and income from other sources, such as vending machines, parking fees, and the like. Even the term *rent* takes into account several different possible figures, as will be considered next.

Rents

Even though a building may be fully occupied by reliable, long-term tenants, the appraiser must consider not only the present rents paid, but also past rents as well as rents currently paid for comparable properties in the area.

Rent currently being paid by agreement between tenant and landlord is called scheduled rent or contract rent. For income properties such as stores, offices, and warehouses, scheduled rent is usually stated as the rent per square foot per year. The usual practice in stating apartment rents is to quote the scheduled rent per unit per year, which then is broken down to the rent per room per year. The appraiser's data on scheduled rent usually comes from the lessee (the tenant, the person renting the property), the lessor (the landlord, the owner of the property), or the real estate agent who manages the property or who may have handled a recent sale.

Market rent is the appraiser's estimate of a property's rent potential. Market rent is the rent the property can be expected to command in the current market, considering what tenants have paid and are paying for the subject property and other comparable properties. Market rent is not necessarily the rent paid by current tenants.

The appraiser will also be interested in **historical rent,** which is the rent paid in past years. Historical rent data for both the subject property and similar properties will tell the appraiser whether the market appears to be following a trend and whether current rent information is likely to be reliable. Again, the appraiser can acquire the needed data from the tenant, landlord, or real estate broker or perhaps from the appraiser's own files.

Other Income

Rents may not be the only source of income. Even a small apartment building may provide coin-operated laundry machines, an amenity that appeals to tenants. Office buildings may offer food and other vending machines, and in larger buildings, the lessor may operate a newspaper stand or convenience store on the premises. A parking area may provide substantial additional income. Any income received must be taken into consideration, because it will be a factor in determining market value.

In making up a statement of potential gross income, the appraiser will list rent and nonrent income separately, then total them. Because the appraiser is itemizing *potential* gross income, the total will very likely be somewhat higher than the actual rent income received for the current year. At this point, for instance, the appraiser totals the expected rent income from all rental units, even though some units may be vacant and some tenants may be in arrears in payment of rent. The appraiser must also include in the potential gross income calculation the rental value of any owner-occupied areas or caretaker's quarters. The value of the use of these areas, even if the current occupant does not pay rent, must be considered.

Income data received from the property owner should always be verified by the tenants, real estate broker, or rental agent.

Effective Gross Income

At this point, the appraiser makes an adjustment to the potential gross income to allow for the fact that the rental units will probably not be fully occupied 100 percent of the time, and some tenants will be slow or will fail to pay the scheduled rent. To derive **effective gross income,** the appraiser must estimate a reasonable percentage of income to represent **vacancy and collection losses** that can be expected to occur over the course of a year, and subtract that amount from potential gross income. Factors to be taken into account include the following:

- Present and past rental losses of the property
- Present and past rental levels for other properties in the area that are in competition with the subject property
- Area population and economic trends
- Reliability of tenants
- Length of existing leases

Under ordinary market conditions (neither boom nor bust), the allowance for vacancy and collection losses is typically in the 5- to 10-percent range. If the area has experienced any amount of overbuilding or for whatever reason has much more property available than current market demand warrants, the vacancy factor may be considerably higher. If the area's economy is experiencing a recession or depression, collection losses as well as vacancies will tend to be higher than normal. On the other hand, if there is a heavier-than-normal demand for space relative to the number of available properties, the appraiser may determine that a lower allowance for vacancy and collection losses is indicated.

Net Operating Income

Having found the effective gross income, the appraiser can deduct the property's operating expenses to derive the **net operating income. Operating expenses** are those costs incurred to maintain the property and to continue the income stream. Such costs include employee salaries and benefits, utility payments, management fees, legal and accounting fees, insurance, and real estate taxes. Other costs are also considered for appraisal purposes but are not considered for accounting purposes, and vice versa. Operating expenses for appraisal purposes include **reserves for replacement,** the fund that is accumulated so that major expenditures for the replacement of building components can be made, but the payments themselves as they are made are not considered operating expenses for appraisal purposes.

Although they are an important part of the accountant's calculation, for appraisal purposes, operating expenses do *not* include the costs to the owner to finance the purchase. The appraiser also does not take into account building depreciation deductions, which may have substantial income tax impact for the property owner. The appraiser is interested in the property's value as an income producer, apart from any effect its ownership may have on a particular investor's after-tax cash flow.

Reconstructing the Operating Statement

The appraiser's estimates and computations are summarized in an **operating statement** for the property being appraised. Because the appraiser's operating statement will include some important differences from the accountant's operating statement for the same property, this process is referred to as **reconstructing the operating statement.** Figure 10.1 is an example of a reconstructed operating statement that shows the accountant's figures as well as the appraiser's calculations.

For the example in Figure 10.1, the appraiser considered the past, present, and expected future rental performance of an eight-unit apartment building. Present income was adjusted upward to reflect the rental value of an apartment occupied by the owner. Vacancy and collection losses, based on an area study, were estimated at five percent of the rental income. The owner uses the services of a part-time custodian and a part-time gardener. Roof replacement is expected every 20 years at a cost of $20,000, requiring a reserve fund of $1,000 per year. Plumbing and electrical replacements are based on a 20-year service life for fixtures costing $30,000, requiring a reserve fund of $1,500 per year. The appraiser will not include the following:

- Payments for capital improvements, such as air conditioners
- Principal and mortgage interest payments, because the property is being appraised on a free and clear basis
- Depreciation, which is calculated by the accountant on the basis of the depreciation schedule allowed by the IRS for federal income tax purposes

Figure 10.1 Operating Statement

	Accountant's Figures	Appraiser's Adjusted Estimate
Gross Income (Rent)	$87,000.00	$92,000
Allowance for Vacancies and Bad Debts	—	4,600
Effective Gross Income	—	87,400
Operating Expenses		
Salaries and wages	12,000.00	12,000
Variable Expenses		
Employees' benefits	1,847.32	1,900
Electricity	1,464.50	1,500
Gas	4,323.00	4,300
Water	700.10	700
Painting and decorating	1,600.00	1,600
Supplies	938.79	900
Repairs	3,530.00	3,500
Management	5,000.00	5,000
Legal and accounting fees	1,500.00	1,500
Payments on air conditioners	1,600.00	—
Miscellaneous expenses	600.00	600
Fixed Expenses		
Insurance (three-year policy)	4,200.00	4,200
Real estate taxes	7,000.00	7,000
Reserves for Replacement		
Roof replacement	—	1,000
Plumbing and electrical	—	1,500
Principal on mortgage	1,800.00	—
Interest on mortgage	18,945.00	—
Depreciation—building	12,000.00	—
Total Expenses	$79,048.71	$47,200
Net Operating Income	$ 7,951.29	$40,200

SELECTING THE CAPITALIZATION RATE

The average investor will expect an income-producing property to provide both a return *on* the investment (profit on the amount invested) and a return *of* the investment (the amount invested). The real estate investment shares the same basic rationale as any investment. The first investment most people make is to deposit cash in a bank account. The depositor expects to earn a certain rate of interest on the funds deposited, which can be withdrawn or left in the account to accumulate additional interest. The depositor also expects to be able to withdraw the principal, the original amount invested. These are the same types of considerations that guide investments in real estate.

The overall rate of return that the investor in real estate receives is called the **capitalization rate** or **overall capitalization rate.** In equation form, it can be expressed as follows:

$$\frac{\text{Net Operating Income}}{\text{Value}} = \text{Capitalization Rate}$$

$$\text{or, } \frac{I}{V} = R$$

The formula for the capitalization rate is particularly useful because of its two corollaries:

1. Capitalization Rate × Value = Net Operating Income, or R × V = I

2. $\dfrac{\text{Net Operating Income}}{\text{Capitalization Rate}} = \text{Value}$

   $$\text{or, } \frac{I}{R} = V$$

Direct Capitalization

The capitalization rate can be developed by evaluating net income figures and sales prices of comparable properties. This process is called direct capitalization. For example, if a comparable property that sold recently for $250,000 produces an income of $25,000 per year, it has a capitalization rate of .10, or 10 percent, using the formula $\frac{I}{V} = R$, and dividing $25,000 by $250,000. To find the value of the subject property, the income that the appraiser estimates the subject property will produce is divided by the capitalization rate of 10 percent. In this case, using the formula $\frac{I}{R} = V$, the subject property's income of $32,000 is divided by 10 percent to derive a value opinion of $320,000.

Yield Capitalization

Yield capitalization is a way of analyzing both components of the capitalization rate (return *on* the investment and return *of* the investment) separately. It is too complex to discuss here, but is worth mentioning because it is likely to be the method of choice for analyzing a large-scale, income-producing property.

Using yield capitalization, the appraiser estimates the income that the property may be expected to produce in the future, then estimates the present worth of the right to receive that income. The appraiser develops a capitalization rate based on the typical investor's required return and applies that rate to the present value of the income stream to derive market value.

SELECTING THE CAPITALIZATION TECHNIQUE

With the property's net operating income and the investor's desired capitalization rate determined, the appropriate capitalization technique must be selected and applied.

The appraiser can first determine the value of the underlying land by using the sales comparison approach, then apply the **building residual technique.** If the appraiser has already computed the building value, the calculations are reversed to find the total property value using the **land residual technique.** Using the **property residual technique,** the property is valued as a whole, including both land and buildings. A factor called an annuity factor, representing the present worth of an investment at the required yield, is multiplied by the net operating income to find the present worth of the income stream.

Figure 10.2 shows examples of how each of the capitalization techniques can be used. Note that each example makes use of a different property, with different income and other variables.

Figure 10.2 Capitalization Techniques

Building Residual Technique			
Estimated Land Value			$ 90,000
Net Operating Income		$40,000	
Discount on Land Value ($90,000 × .12)		− 10,800	
Residual Income to Building		$29,200	
Capitalization Rate for Building			
Discount Rate	12%		
Recapture Rate	+ 5%		
	17%		
Building Value ($29,200 ÷ .17)			171,800
Total Property Value			$261,800
Land Residual Technique			
Assumed Building Value			$325,000
Net Operating Income		$65,000	
Capitalization Rate for Building			
Discount Rate	11.875%		
Recapture Rate	+ 4.000%		
	15.875%		
Discount and Recapture on Building			
Value ($325,000 × .15875)		− 51,600	
Residual Income to Land		$13,400	
Land Value ($13,400 ÷ .11875)			112,800
Total Property Value			$437,800
Property Residual Technique			
Total Annual Net Operating Income			$ 40,000
Annuity Factor (23 years at 13%)			7.230
Present Worth of Net Operating Income			$289,200

GROSS INCOME MULTIPLIER

Even though the income approach can be very detailed and can require a knowledge of sophisticated accounting techniques, a much simpler form of income analysis can be used to develop an opinion of market value.

For single-family residences, the gross income used will be the amount of the monthly rent, with no other source of income from the property. For this reason, this approach may be referred to as the gross rent multiplier (GRM) method. When appraising commercial and industrial properties, the amount of annual income from all sources is likely to include more than just rents, and the **gross income multiplier (GIM)** is the more appropriate term.

The theory behind the use of the GIM or GRM is that rental prices and sales prices generally react to the same market influences, and so they tend to move in the same direction. Of course, not all factors will affect both rental prices and sales prices equally or at the same time. If property taxes go up, rents may rise well ahead of the time that the taxed property is sold. If a sudden drop in demand for rental units occurs because of overbuilding, rental prices and sales prices will both drop as new leases are begun and sales occur.

Some tenants are fortunate because they are paying rents based on the present owner's costs, which may be substantially less than those a new owner would incur to pay for the same property at today's prices. The appraiser should analyze the rental and sales prices of properties comparable to the property being appraised, keeping in mind the same economic factors that generally contribute to market value.

The relationship between the sales price and rental price can be expressed as a factor or ratio, which is the gross income or gross rent multiplier. The ratio is expressed as follows:

$$\frac{\text{Sales Price}}{\text{Gross Income}} = \text{GIM or} \frac{\text{Sales Price}}{\text{Gross Rent}} = \text{GRM}$$

To establish a reasonably accurate GRM, the appraiser should have recent sales and rental data from at least 10 properties similar to the subject property that have sold in the same market area and were rented at the time of sale. The resulting GRM can then be applied to the projected rental of the subject property to develop an opinion of its market value. This is done using the following:

$$\text{Gross Rent} \times \text{GRM} = \text{Market Value}$$

The steps in applying the GRM can be summarized as follows:

1. Estimate the subject property's monthly market rent.

2. Calculate GRMs from recently sold comparable properties that were rented at the time of sale.

3. Based on rent multiplier analysis, derive the appropriate GRM for the subject property

4. Develop an opinion of market value by multiplying the amount of the monthly market rent by the subject property's GRM

Figure 10.3 shows how a GRM can be obtained for a single-family residence and applied to the subject property to derive market value. The appraiser's main concern will be to find comparable properties in the area that are being rented. Remember, too, that the appraiser must estimate a fair rental value for the subject property to apply the GRM. This may be difficult if the property contains unique features that make it unlike others on the market.

Figure 10.3 Gross Rent Multiplier

Sale No.	Sales Price	Monthly Rental Income	Gross Rent Multiplier
1	$150,000	$ 975	154
2	145,000	975	149
3	152,000	1,000	152
4	140,000	875	160
5	160,000	1,100	145
Subject	?	1,000	?

In the example in Figure 10.3, the appraiser's GRMs range from 145 to 160. Discounting the high and low ends of the range, the remaining three figures are 149, 152, and 154. Based on the appraiser's knowledge of the properties involved and their similarities to the subject property, the multiplier of 152 is selected as being the most appropriate. The last step is to apply the GRM to the estimated rental value of the subject:

$1,000 × 152 = $152,000, the indicated value of the subject property by the
income approach

In summary, if the right kinds of data are available to develop valid market rent and GRM estimates, the income approach for single-family residences can be used, if only to serve as a check against the sales comparison and cost approaches.

Income Approach Using the URAR Form

In the income approach section of the Uniform Residential Appraisal Report (URAR), the appraiser must do the following:

1. Enter the subject property's monthly market rent estimate derived from the marketplace.

2. Enter the GRM applicable to the subject property.

3. Multiply the monthly market rent estimate by the GRM.

4. Enter the value estimate indicated by the income approach.

Figure 10.4 Income Approach Section of the URAR Form

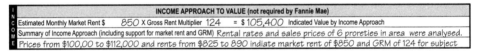

INCOME APPROACH TO VALUE (not required by Fannie Mae)
Estimated Monthly Market Rent $ 850 X Gross Rent Multiplier 124   = $ 105,400   Indicated Value by Income Approach
Summary of Income Approach (including support for market rent and GRM) Rental rates and sales prices of 6 proreties in area were analysed.
Prices from $100,00 to $112,000 and rents from $825 to 890 indiate market rent of $850 and GRM of 124 for subject

APPRAISAL WORKSHEET

1. Is the subject property currently being rented, and if it is, what is the amount of the monthly rent?_____

2. Are comparable properties in the area currently being rented?_____

3. In the chart that follows, try to list at least five properties from the area that are comparable to the subject property, are used as rentals, and have been sold recently.

Sale No.	Sales Price	Monthly Rental Income	Gross Rent Multiplier
1			
2			
3			
4			
5			

4. For each comparable property listed in the chart, divide the sales price by the amount of the monthly rent, and enter the resulting GRM in the chart.

5. Select the GRM that is most appropriate for the subject property. _____

6. Based on the rents charged for properties comparable to the subject property, estimate the amount of rent that could be charged for the subject property. _____

7. Multiply the estimated rent for the property by the GRM that you selected as most appropriate to develop your opinion of market value. _____

Reconciliation and the Appraisal Report

11

The last step in the appraisal process, before the final report is prepared, is the reconciliation of the values indicated by each of the three appraisal approaches. Using the cost approach, the cost of reproducing or replacing the structure less depreciation plus site value has been calculated. With the income approach, value has been based on income the property should be capable of producing. With the sales comparison approach, the analysis of comparable sales produced adjusted sales prices that were used to derive an opinion of value for the subject property.

RECONCILIATION

The value opinions reached by using the different approaches will rarely be exactly the same. Even if the appraiser had all the relevant data and had carried out the steps in each approach without error, each value indication, in almost every case, would be different. In the **reconciliation** process, the validity of the methods and the result of each approach are weighed objectively to arrive at the single best and most supportable conclusion of value. This process also is called correlation.

In reconciling, or correlating, the appraiser reviews his or her work and considers at least the following four factors:

1. Definition of value sought
2. Amount and reliability of the data collected in each approach
3. Inherent strengths and weaknesses of each approach
4. Relevance of each approach to the subject property and market behavior

The process of reconciliation is not a simple averaging of the differing value estimates. After the factors listed previously are considered, the most relevant approach—cost, sales comparison, or income—receives the greatest weight when

177

determining the value opinion that most accurately reflects the value sought. In addition, each approach serves as a check against the others.

Review of the Three Approaches

To begin the reconciliation process, the appraiser reviews the steps followed in each approach to substantiate the accuracy and consistency of all data and the logic leading to the value opinion. The checklists in Figures 11.1 through 11.4 can be used to review each valuation approach.

Weighing the Choices

Once the appraiser is assured of the validity of the indicated values, the appraiser then must decide which is the most reliable, in terms of the value sought, for the subject property. Inherent factors may make a particular method automatically more significant for certain kinds of property (such as the income approach for investment properties or the cost approach for special purpose properties). But other factors, of which the appraiser should be aware, may negate part of that significance. An unstable neighborhood, for instance, may make any structure virtually worthless. If the appraiser is trying to arrive at an opinion of market value, and if the market for property in a certain neighborhood is likely to be extremely small, the appraiser should reflect this fact in his or her final opinion of value.

Figure 11.1 Checklist for Sales Comparison Approach

Check:

_____ 1. That properties selected as comparables are sufficiently similar to the subject property

_____ 2. Amount and reliability of sales data

_____ 3. Factors used in comparison

_____ 4. Logic of the adjustments made between comparable sales properties and the subject property

_____ 5. Soundness of the value derived from the adjusted sales prices of comparable properties

_____ 6. Mathematical accuracy of the adjustment computations

A check of all mathematical calculations is an important part of the review process because errors can lead to incorrect value indications and can destroy the credibility of the entire appraisal.

Figure 11.2 Checklist for Cost Approach

Check:

_____ 1.   That sites used as comparables are, in fact, similar to the subject site

_____ 2.   Amount and reliability of the comparable sales data collected

_____ 3.   Appropriateness of the factors used in comparison

_____ 4.   Logic of the adjustments made between comparable sales sites and the subject site

_____ 5.   Soundness of the value derived from the adjusted sales prices of comparable sites

_____ 6.   Mathematical accuracy of the adjustment computations

_____ 7.   Appropriateness of the method of estimating reproduction or replacement cost

_____ 8.   Appropriateness of the unit cost factor

_____ 9.   Accuracy of the reproduction or replacement cost computations

_____ 10. Market values assigned to accrued depreciation charges

_____ 11. For double counting and/or omissions in making accrued depreciation charges

---

Figure 11.3 Checklist for Income Capitalization Approach

Check the logic and the mathematical accuracy of the following:

_____ 1.   Market rents

_____ 2.   Potential gross income estimate

_____ 3.   Allowance for vacancy and collection losses

_____ 4.   Operating expense estimate, including reserves for replacement

_____ 5.   Net income estimate

_____ 6.   Estimate of remaining economic life

_____ 7.   Capitalization rate and method of capitalizing

Figure 11.4 Checklist for Gross Rent Multiplier Method

Check:

_____ 1.   That properties analyzed are comparable to the subject property and to one another in terms of locational, physical, and investment characteristics

_____ 2.   That adequate rental data is available

_____ 3.   That comparable sales were drawn from properties that were rented at the time of sale

_____ 4.   That the gross rent multiplier for the subject property was derived from current sales and current rental incomes

_____ 5.   Mathematical accuracy of all computations

Example

An appraiser forming an opinion of the market value of a home in a neighborhood composed predominantly of owner-occupied, single-family houses arrived at the following initial figures:

Sales comparison approach	$365,750
Cost approach	373,000
Income approach	369,400

Based on these indications of value, the range is from $365,750 to $373,000, a difference of $7,250 between the lowest indication of value and the highest. This relatively narrow range suggests that the information gathered and analyzed is a reasonable and reliable representation of the market.

When reviewing the data collected for the sales comparison approach and the results drawn, the appraiser realized that an opinion of value based on this information should be very reliable. Other houses in the same general condition and with the same types of improvements were selling from $362,000 to $371,000. Because all comparable sales used in the analysis required few adjustments, considerable weight was given to the sales comparison approach, as normally would be expected. After allowing for specific differences, an indicated value of $365,750 was determined for the subject property by applying the sales comparison approach.

Next, the appraiser analyzed the information collected and the result obtained using the cost approach. The cost approach tends to set an upper limit of value when the property is new, without functional or external obsolescence, and at its highest and best use. The older a structure becomes, however, the more difficult it is to accurately estimate the proper amount of accrued depreciation. The fact that the house is relatively new, only a few years old, strengthens the $373,000 opinion of value by the cost approach.

Finally, the appraiser considered the market value derived from the income approach. This approach seemed to be the least valid for this particular property because few houses in the subject neighborhood are rentals and even fewer rental homes have been sold currently, making it difficult to establish a reasonably accurate GRM.

As stated previously, the final opinion of value is not an average but an opinion that the appraiser makes based on the type of property being appraised, the results of the research compiled, and the valuation techniques used. In this case, the appraiser placed the most weight on the sales comparison approach.

The appraiser's final opinion of market value for the property is $365,750.

Summary

The reconciliation process can be summarized best by a discussion of what it is *not*. Value reconciliation is *not* the correction of errors in thinking and technique. Any corrections to be made are actually part of the review process that preceded the final conclusion of value. The appraiser reconsiders the reasons for the various choices that were made throughout the appraisal framework as they affect the value reached by the three approaches.

No formula exists for reconciling the various indicated values. Rather, reconciliation involves applying careful analysis and judgment for which no mathematical or mechanical formula can be substituted.

Reconciliation is also not merely a matter of averaging the three values. Using a simple arithmetical average implies that the data and logic applied in each of the three approaches are equally reliable and therefore should be given equal weight. Certain approaches are obviously more valid and reliable with some kinds of properties than with others.

Finally, value reconciliation is not a narrowing of the range of values reached by the three appraisal approaches. Those values are never changed—unless an error is found. Reconciliation is the final statement of reasoning and weighing of the relative importance of the facts, results, and conclusions of each of the approaches that culminates in a fully justified final opinion of market value.

TYPES OF APPRAISAL REPORTS

The Uniform Standards of Professional Appraisal Practice (USPAP) permits three types of appraisal reports:

1. *Self-contained report.* This report is a thorough presentation of the data, analyses, and reasoning that have led to the appraiser's opinion of value.

2. *Summary report.* Though not as complete as a self-contained report, the summary report must contain sufficient information to lead the client to the appraiser's conclusion. The URAR form is a summary report.

3. *Restricted use report.* This report is made for a specific client and for a stated limited purpose. Because the restricted use report contains virtually none of the information the appraiser used to arrive at the opinion of value, it is rarely used.

The appraiser can report the final opinion of value to the client in basically two ways: a form report or a narrative appraisal report.

A form report makes use of a standard form to provide, in a few pages, a synopsis of the data supporting the conclusion of value. The report form is usually accompanied by one or more exhibits. These include location and plat maps, plot and floor plans, and photographs of the subject property and comparables. The type of property as well as the definition of the value sought will determine the exact form to be used.

In the secondary mortgage market created by government-supervised corporations and private organizations, form reports are required for the purchase and sale of most existing mortgages on residential properties. Figure 11.5 shows the six-page Uniform Residential Appraisal Report (URAR) form commonly used by appraisers when valuing homes.

The most thorough presentation of the appraiser's assumptions, data, analyses, findings, and conclusions is provided in a narrative appraisal report. In a narrative appraisal report, the appraiser summarizes the important background research and presents all the relevant data for each appraisal method that contributed to the final opinion of value. A number of exhibits may be included, such as photographs of the subject property and its comparables and maps showing demographic, topographical, soil, and other analyses of the subject and its comparables. Narrative reports can contain just a few pages to several hundred pages.

Every appraisal report, regardless of its length, should contain the following six items:

1. Name of person for whom the report is made
2. Date of appraisal
3. Identification and description of the property
4. Purpose of the appraisal
5. Value conclusion
6. Appraiser's certification and signature

FINAL COMMENT

It should be obvious to the reader that an appraiser is not a magician and does not consult a crystal ball to forecast property value.

Remember that an appraisal is not an exercise in stargazing or fortune-telling, but a process that should lead to a well-reasoned judgment based on available facts.

Figure 11.5 Uniform Residential Appraisal Report Form

Uniform Residential Appraisal Report   File

The purpose of this summary appraisal report is to provide the lender/client with an accurate, and adequately supported, opinion of the market value of the subject property.

S U B J E C T

Property Address		City		State	Zip Code
Borrower	Owner of Public Record			County	

Legal Description

Assessor's Parcel #		Tax Year	R.E. Taxes $

Neighborhood Name		Map Reference	Census Tract

Occupant ☐ Owner ☐ Tenant ☐ Vacant   Special Assessments $ ☐ PUD   HOA $ ☐ per year ☐ per month

Property Rights Appraised ☐ Fee Simple ☐ Leasehold ☐ Other (describe)

Assignment Type ☐ Purchase Transaction ☐ Refinance Transaction ☐ Other (describe)

Lender/Client   Address

Is the subject property currently offered for sale or has it been offered for sale in the twelve months prior to the effective   date of this appraisal? ☐ Yes ☐ No

Report data source(s) used, offering price(s), and date(s).

C O N T R A C T

I ☐ did ☐ did not analyze the contract for sale for the subject purchase transaction. Explain the results of the analysis of the contrac t for sale or why the analysis was not performed.

Contract Price $ Date of Contract   Is the property seller the owner of public record? ☐ Yes ☐ No Data Source(s)

Is there any financial assistance (loan charges, sale concessions, gift or downpayment assistance, etc.) to be paid by any part y on behalf of the borrower? ☐ Yes ☐ No
If Yes, report the total dollar amount and describe the items to be paid.

N E I G H B O R H O O D

Note: Race and the racial composition of the neighborhood are not appraisal factors.

Neighborhood Characteristics			One-Unit Housing Trends			One-Unit Housing		Present Land Use %	
Location ☐ Urban ☐ Suburban ☐ Rural			Property Values ☐ Increasing ☐ Stable ☐ Declining			PRICE	AGE	One-Unit	%
Built-Up ☐ Over 75% ☐ 25–75% ☐ Under 25%			Demand/Supply ☐ Shortage ☐ In Balance ☐ Over Supply			$ (000)	(yrs)	2-4 Unit	%
Growth ☐ Rapid ☐ Stable ☐ Slow			Marketing Time ☐ Under 3 mths ☐ 3–6 mths ☐ Over 6 mths			Low		Multi-Family	%
Neighborhood Boundaries						High		Commercial	%
						Pred.		Other	%

Neighborhood Description

Market Conditions (including support for the above conclusions)

S I T E

Dimensions		Area	Shape		View	

Specific Zoning Classification   Zoning Description

Zoning Compliance ☐ Legal ☐ Legal Nonconforming (Grandfathered Use) ☐ No Zoning ☐ Illegal (describe)

Is the highest and best use of the subject property as improved (or as proposed per plans and specifications) the present use? ☐ Yes ☐ No If No, describe

Utilities	Public	Other (describe)		Public	Other (describe)	Off-site Improvements—Type	Public	Private
Electricity	☐	☐	Water	☐	☐	Street	☐	☐
Gas	☐	☐	Sanitary Sewer	☐	☐	Alley	☐	☐

FEMA Special Flood Hazard Area ☐ Yes ☐ No FEMA Flood Zone   FEMA Map #   FEMA Map Date

Are the utilities and off-site improvements typical for the market area? ☐ Yes ☐ No If No, describe

Are there any adverse site conditions or external factors (easements, encroachments, environmental conditions, land uses, etc.) ? ☐ Yes ☐ No If Yes, describe

I M P R O V E M E N T S

General Description		Foundation		Exterior Description materials/condition		Interior materials/condition	
Units ☐ One ☐ One with Accessory Unit		☐ Concrete Slab ☐ Crawl Space		Foundation Walls		Floors	
# of Stories		☐ Full Basement ☐ Partial Basement		Exterior Walls		Walls	
Type ☐ Det. ☐ Att. ☐ S-Det./End Unit		Basement Area sq. ft.		Roof Surface		Trim/Finish	
☐ Existing ☐ Proposed ☐ Under Const.		Basement Finish %		Gutters & Downspouts		Bath Floor	
Design (Style)		☐ Outside Entry/Exit ☐ Sump Pump		Window Type		Bath Wainscot	
Year Built		Evidence of ☐ Infestation		Storm Sash/Insulated		Car Storage ☐ None	
Effective Age (Yrs)		☐ Dampness ☐ Settlement		Screens		☐ Driveway # of Cars	
Attic ☐ None		Heating ☐ FWA ☐ HWBB ☐ Radiant		Amenities ☐ Woodstove(s) #		Driveway Surface	
☐ Drop Stair ☐ Stairs		☐ Other Fuel		☐ Fireplace(s) # ☐ Fence		☐ Garage # of Cars	
☐ Floor ☐ Scuttle		Cooling ☐ Central Air Conditioning		☐ Patio/Deck ☐ Porch		☐ Carport # of Cars	
☐ Finished ☐ Heated		☐ Individual ☐ Other		☐ Pool ☐ Other		☐ Att. ☐ Det. ☐ Built-in	

Appliances ☐ Refrigerator ☐ Range/Oven ☐ Dishwasher ☐ Disposal ☐ Microwave ☐ Washer/Dryer ☐ Other (describe)

Finished area **above** grade contains: Rooms   Bedrooms   Bath(s)   Square Feet of Gross Living Area Above Grade

Additional features (special energy efficient items, etc.)

Describe the condition of the property (including needed repairs, deterioration, renovations, remodeling, etc.).

Are there any physical deficiencies or adverse conditions that affect the livability, soundness, or structural integrity of the property? ☐ Yes ☐ No If Yes, describe

Does the property generally conform to the neighborhood (functional utility, style, condition, use, construction, etc.)? ☐ Yes ☐ No If No, describe

Uniform Residential Appraisal Report

File #

| There are | comparable properties currently offered for sale in the subject neighborhood ranging in price from $ | | | | | to $ | | |

| There are | comparable sales in the subject neighborhood within the past twelve months ranging in sale price from $ | | | | | to $ | | |

FEATURE	SUBJECT	COMPARABLE SALE # 1		COMPARABLE SALE # 2		COMPARABLE SALE # 3	
Address							
Proximity to Subject							
Sale Price	$		$		$		$
Sale Price/Gross Liv. Area	$ sq. ft.	$ sq. ft.		$ sq. ft.		$ sq. ft.	
Data Source(s)							
Verification Source(s)							
VALUE ADJUSTMENTS	DESCRIPTION	DESCRIPTION	+(-) $ Adjustment	DESCRIPTION	+(-) $ Adjustment	DESCRIPTION	+(-) $ Adjustment
Sale or Financing Concessions							
Date of Sale/Time							
Location							
Leasehold/Fee Simple							
Site							
View							
Design (Style)							
Quality of Construction							
Actual Age							
Condition							
Above Grade	Total Bdrms. Baths	Total Bdrms. Baths		Total Bdrms. Baths		Total Bdrms. Baths	
Room Count							
Gross Living Area	sq. ft.	sq. ft.		sq. ft.		sq. ft.	
Basement & Finished Rooms Below Grade							
Functional Utility							
Heating/Cooling							
Energy Efficient Items							
Garage/Carport							
Porch/Patio/Deck							
Net Adjustment (Total)		☐ + ☐ -	$	☐ + ☐ -	$	☐ + ☐ -	$
Adjusted Sale Price of Comparables		Net Adj. % Gross Adj. %	$	Net Adj. % Gross Adj. %	$	Net Adj. % Gross Adj. %	$

I ☐ did ☐ did not research the sale or transfer history of the subject property and comparable sales. If not, explain

My research ☐ did ☐ did not reveal any prior sales or transfers of the subject property for the three years prior to the effective date of this appraisal.

Data source(s)

My research ☐ did ☐ did not reveal any prior sales or transfers of the comparable sales for the year prior to the date of sale of the comparable sale.

Data source(s)

Report the results of the research and analysis of the prior sale or transfer history of the subject property and comparable sales (report additional prior sales on page 3).

ITEM	SUBJECT	COMPARABLE SALE # 1	COMPARABLE SALE # 2	COMPARABLE SALE # 3
Date of Prior Sale/Transfer				
Price of Prior Sale/Transfer				
Data Source(s)				
Effective Date of Data Source(s)				

Analysis of prior sale or transfer history of the subject property and comparable sales

Summary of Sales Comparison Approach

Indicated Value by Sales Comparison Approach $

Indicated Value by: Sales Comparison Approach $ Cost Approach (if developed) $ Income Approach (if developed) $

This appraisal is made ☐ "as is", ☐ subject to completion per plans and specifications on the basis of a hypothetical condition that the improvements have been completed, ☐ subject to the following repairs or alterations on the basis of a hypothetical condition that the repairs or alterations have been completed, or ☐ subject to the following required inspection based on the extraordinary assumption that the condition or deficiency does not require alteration or repair:

Based on a complete visual inspection of the interior and exterior areas of the subject property, defined scope of work, statement of assumptions and limiting conditions, and appraiser's certification, my (our) opinion of the market value, as defined, of the real property that is the subject of this report is
$, as of   , which is the date of inspection and the effective date of this appraisal.

Uniform Residential Appraisal Report   File

ADDITIONAL COMMENTS

COST APPROACH TO VALUE (not required by Fannie Mae)

Provide adequate information for the lender/client to replicate the below cost figures and calculations.

Support for the opinion of site value (summary of comparable land sales or other methods for estimating site value)

COST APPROACH

ESTIMATED ☐ REPRODUCTION OR ☐ REPLACEMENT COST NEW	OPINION OF SITE VALUE .... = $
Source of cost data	Dwelling Sq. Ft. @ $ =$
Quality rating from cost service Effective date of cost data	Sq. Ft. @ $ =$
Comments on Cost Approach (gross living area calculations, depreciation, etc.)	Garage/Carport Sq. Ft. @ $ =$
	Total Estimate of Cost-New = $
	Less Physical Functional External
	Depreciation =$( )
	Depreciated Cost of Improvements.....................=$
	"As-is" Value of Site Improvements.....................=$
Estimated Remaining Economic Life (HUD and VA only) Years	Indicated Value By Cost Approach ....=$

INCOME APPROACH TO VALUE (not required by Fannie Mae)

INCOME

Estimated Monthly Market Rent $ X Gross Rent Multiplier = $ Indicated Value by Income Approach	
Summary of Income Approach (including support for market rent and GRM)	

PROJECT INFORMATION FOR PUDs (if applicable)

PUD INFORMATION

Is the developer/builder in control of the Homeowners' Association (HOA)? ☐ Yes ☐ No   Unit type(s) ☐ Detached ☐ Attached

Provide the following information for PUDs ONLY if the developer/builder is in control of the HOA and the subject property is an attached dwelling unit.

Legal name of project

Total number of phases   Total number of units   Total number of units sold

Total number of units rented   Total number of units for sale   Data source(s)

Was the project created by the conversion of an existing building(s) into a PUD? ☐ Yes ☐ No   If Yes, date of conversion

Does the project contain any multi-dwelling units? ☐ Yes ☐ No   Data source(s)

Are the units, common elements, and recreation facilities complete? ☐ Yes ☐ No   If No, describe the status of completion.

Are the common elements leased to or by the Homeowners' Association? ☐ Yes ☐ No   If Yes, describe the rental terms and options.

Describe common elements and recreational facilities

Uniform Residential Appraisal Report   File

This report form is designed to report an appraisal of a one-unit property or a one-unit property with an accessory unit; including a unit in a planned unit development (PUD). This report form is not designed to report an appraisal of a manufactured home or a unit in a condominium or cooperative project.

This appraisal report is subject to the following scope of work, intended use, intended user, definition of market value, statement of assumptions and limiting conditions, and certifications. Modifications, additions, or deletions to the intended use, intended user, definition of market value, or assumptions and limiting conditions are not permitted. The appraiser may expand the scope of work to include any additional research or analysis necessary based on the complexity of this appraisal assignment. Modifications or deletions to the certifications are also not permitted. However, additional certifications that do not constitute material alterations to this appraisal report, such as those required by law or those related to the appraiser's continuing education or membership in an appraisal organization, are permitted.

SCOPE OF WORK: The scope of work for this appraisal is defined by the complexity of this appraisal assignment and the reporting requirements of this appraisal report form, including the following definition of market value, statement of assumptions and limiting conditions, and certifications. The appraiser must, at a minimum: (1) perform a complete visual inspection of the interior and exterior areas of the subject property, (2) inspect the neighborhood, (3) inspect each of the comparable sales from at least the street, (4) research, verify, and analyze data from reliable public and/or private sources, and (5) report his or her analysis, opinions, and conclusions in this appraisal report.

INTENDED USE: The intended use of this appraisal report is for the lender/client to evaluate the property that is the subject of this appraisal for a mortgage finance transaction.

INTENDED USER: The intended user of this appraisal report is the lender/client.

DEFINITION OF MARKET VALUE: The most probable price which a property should bring in a competitive and open market under all conditions requisite to a fair sale, the buyer and seller, each acting prudently, knowledgeably and assuming the price is not affected by undue stimulus. Implicit in this definition is the consummation of a sale as of a specified date and the passing of title from seller to buyer under conditions whereby: (1) buyer and seller are typically motivated; (2) both parties are well informed or well advised, and each acting in what he or she considers his or her own best interest; (3) a reasonable time is allowed for exposure in the open market; (4) payment is made in terms of cash in U. S. dollars or in terms of financial arrangements comparable thereto; and (5) the price represents the normal consideration for the property sold unaffected by special or creative financing or sales concessions* granted by anyone associated with the sale.

*Adjustments to the comparables must be made for special or creative financing or sales concessions. No adjustments are necessary for those costs which are normally paid by sellers as a result of tradition or law in a market area; these costs are readily identifiable since the seller pays these costs in virtually all sales transactions. Special or creative financing adjustments can be made to the comparable property by comparisons to financing terms offered by a third party institutional lender that is not already involved in the property or transaction. Any adjustment should not be calculated on a mechanical dollar for dollar cost of the financing or concession but the dollar amount of any adjustment should approximate the market's reaction to the financing or concessions based on the appraiser's judgment.

STATEMENT OF ASSUMPTIONS AND LIMITING CONDITIONS: The appraiser's certification in this report is subject to the following assumptions and limiting conditions:

1. The appraiser will not be responsible for matters of a legal nature that affect either the property being appraised or the title to it, except for information that he or she became aware of during the research involved in performing this appraisal. The appraiser assumes that the title is good and marketable and will not render any opinions about the title.

2. The appraiser has provided a sketch in this appraisal report to show the approximate dimensions of the improvements. The sketch is included only to assist the reader in visualizing the property and understanding the appraiser's determination of its size.

3. The appraiser has examined the available flood maps that are provided by the Federal Emergency Management Agency (or other data sources) and has noted in this appraisal report whether any portion of the subject site is located in an identified Special Flood Hazard Area. Because the appraiser is not a surveyor, he or she makes no guarantees, express or implied, regarding this determination.

4. The appraiser will not give testimony or appear in court because he or she made an appraisal of the property in question, unless specific arrangements to do so have been made beforehand, or as otherwise required by law.

5. The appraiser has noted in this appraisal report any adverse conditions (such as needed repairs, deterioration, the presence of hazardous wastes, toxic substances, etc.) observed during the inspection of the subject property or that he or she became aware of during the research involved in performing this appraisal. Unless otherwise stated in this appraisal report, the appraiser has no knowledge of any hidden or unapparent physical deficiencies or adverse conditions of the property (such as, but not limited to, needed repairs, deterioration, the presence of hazardous wastes, toxic substances, adverse environmental conditions, etc.) that would make the property less valuable, and has assumed that there are no such conditions and makes no guarantees or warranties, express or implied. The appraiser will not be responsible for any such conditions that do exist or for any engineering or testing that might be required to discover whether such conditions exist. Because the appraiser is not an expert in the field of environmental hazards, this appraisal report must not be considered as an environmental assessment of the property.

6. The appraiser has based his or her appraisal report and valuation conclusion for an appraisal that is subject to satisfactory completion, repairs, or alterations on the assumption that the completion, repairs, or alterations of the subject property will be performed in a professional manner.

Uniform Residential Appraisal Report   File

APPRAISER'S CERTIFICATION: The Appraiser certifies and agrees that:

1. I have, at a minimum, developed and reported this appraisal in accordance with the scope of work requirements stated in this appraisal report.

2. I performed a complete visual inspection of the interior and exterior areas of the subject property. I reported the condition of the improvements in factual, specific terms. I identified and reported the physical deficiencies that could affect the livability, soundness, or structural integrity of the property.

3. I performed this appraisal in accordance with the requirements of the Uniform Standards of Professional Appraisal Practice that were adopted and promulgated by the Appraisal Standards Board of The Appraisal Foundation and that were in place at the time this appraisal report was prepared.

4. I developed my opinion of the market value of the real property that is the subject of this report based on the sales comparison approach to value. I have adequate comparable market data to develop a reliable sales comparison approach for this appraisal assignment. I further certify that I considered the cost and income approaches to value but did not develop them, unless otherwise indicated in this report.

5. I researched, verified, analyzed, and reported on any current agreement for sale for the subject property, any offering for sale of the subject property in the twelve months prior to the effective date of this appraisal, and the prior sales of the subject property for a minimum of three years prior to the effective date of this appraisal, unless otherwise indicated in this report.

6. I researched, verified, analyzed, and reported on the prior sales of the comparable sales for a minimum of one year prior to the date of sale of the comparable sale, unless otherwise indicated in this report.

7. I selected and used comparable sales that are locationally, physically, and functionally the most similar to the subject property.

8. I have not used comparable sales that were the result of combining a land sale with the contract purchase price of a home that has been built or will be built on the land.

9. I have reported adjustments to the comparable sales that reflect the market's reaction to the differences between the subject property and the comparable sales.

10. I verified, from a disinterested source, all information in this report that was provided by parties who have a financial interest in the sale or financing of the subject property.

11. I have knowledge and experience in appraising this type of property in this market area.

12. I am aware of, and have access to, the necessary and appropriate public and private data sources, such as multiple listing services, tax assessment records, public land records and other such data sources for the area in which the property is located.

13. I obtained the information, estimates, and opinions furnished by other parties and expressed in this appraisal report from reliable sources that I believe to be true and correct.

14. I have taken into consideration the factors that have an impact on value with respect to the subject neighborhood, subject property, and the proximity of the subject property to adverse influences in the development of my opinion of market value. I have noted in this appraisal report any adverse conditions (such as, but not limited to, needed repairs, deterioration, the presence of hazardous wastes, toxic substances, adverse environmental conditions, etc.) observed during the inspection of the subject property or that I became aware of during the research involved in performing this appraisal. I have considered these adverse conditions in my analysis of the property value, and have reported on the effect of the conditions on the value and marketability of the subject property.

15. I have not knowingly withheld any significant information from this appraisal report and, to the best of my knowledge, all statements and information in this appraisal report are true and correct.

16. I stated in this appraisal report my own personal, unbiased, and professional analysis, opinions, and conclusions, which are subject only to the assumptions and limiting conditions in this appraisal report.

17. I have no present or prospective interest in the property that is the subject of this report, and I have no present or prospective personal interest or bias with respect to the participants in the transaction. I did not base, either partially or completely, my analysis and/or opinion of market value in this appraisal report on the race, color, religion, sex, age, marital status, handicap, familial status, or national origin of either the prospective owners or occupants of the subject property or of the present owners or occupants of the properties in the vicinity of the subject property or on any other basis prohibited by law.

18. My employment and/or compensation for performing this appraisal or any future or anticipated appraisals was not conditioned on any agreement or understanding, written or otherwise, that I would report (or present analysis supporting) a predetermined specific value, a predetermined minimum value, a range or direction in value, a value that favors the cause of any party, or the attainment of a specific result or occurrence of a specific subsequent event (such as approval of a pending mortgage loan application).

19. I personally prepared all conclusions and opinions about the real estate that were set forth in this appraisal report. If I relied on significant real property appraisal assistance from any individual or individuals in the performance of this appraisal or the preparation of this appraisal report, I have named such individual(s) and disclosed the specific tasks performed in this appraisal report. I certify that any individual so named is qualified to perform the tasks. I have not authorized anyone to make a change to any item in this appraisal report; therefore, any change made to this appraisal is unauthorized and I will take no responsibility for it.

20. I identified the lender/client in this appraisal report who is the individual, organization, or agent for the organization that ordered and will receive this appraisal report.

Uniform Residential Appraisal Report   File

21. The lender/client may disclose or distribute this appraisal report to: the borrower; another lender at the request of the borrower; the mortgagee or its successors and assigns; mortgage insurers; government sponsored enterprises; other secondary market participants; data collection or reporting services; professional appraisal organizations; any department, agency, or instrumentality of the United States; and any state, the District of Columbia, or other jurisdictions; without having to obtain the appraiser's or supervisory appraiser's (if applicable) consent. Such consent must be obtained before this appraisal report may be disclosed or distributed to any other party (including, but not limited to, the public through advertising, public relations, news, sales, or other media).

22. I am aware that any disclosure or distribution of this appraisal report by me or the lender/client may be subject to certain laws and regulations. Further, I am also subject to the provisions of the Uniform Standards of Professional Appraisal Practice that pertain to disclosure or distribution by me.

23. The borrower, another lender at the request of the borrower, the mortgagee or its successors and assigns, mortgage insurers, government sponsored enterprises, and other secondary market participants may rely on this appraisal report as part of any mortgage finance transaction that involves any one or more of these parties.

24. If this appraisal report was transmitted as an "electronic record" containing my "electronic signature," as those terms are defined in applicable federal and/or state laws (excluding audio and video recordings), or a facsimile transmission of this appraisal report containing a copy or representation of my signature, the appraisal report shall be as effective, enforceable and valid as if a paper version of this appraisal report were delivered containing my original hand written signature.

25. Any intentional or negligent misrepresentation(s) contained in this appraisal report may result in civil liability and/or criminal penalties including, but not limited to, fine or imprisonment or both under the provisions of Title 18, United States Code, Section 1001, et seq., or similar state laws.

SUPERVISORY APPRAISER'S CERTIFICATION: The Supervisory Appraiser certifies and agrees that:

1. I directly supervised the appraiser for this appraisal assignment, have read the appraisal report, and agree with the appraiser's analysis, opinions, statements, conclusions, and the appraiser's certification.

2. I accept full responsibility for the contents of this appraisal report including, but not limited to, the appraiser's analysis, opinions, statements, conclusions, and the appraiser's certification.

3. The appraiser identified in this appraisal report is either a sub-contractor or an employee of the supervisory appraiser (or the appraisal firm), is qualified to perform this appraisal, and is acceptable to perform this appraisal under the applicable state law.

4. This appraisal report complies with the Uniform Standards of Professional Appraisal Practice that were adopted and promulgated by the Appraisal Standards Board of The Appraisal Foundation and that were in place at the time this appraisal report was prepared.

5. If this appraisal report was transmitted as an "electronic record" containing my "electronic signature," as those terms are defined in applicable federal and/or state laws (excluding audio and video recordings), or a facsimile transmission of this appraisal report containing a copy or representation of my signature, the appraisal report shall be as effective, enforceable and valid as if a paper version of this appraisal report were delivered containing my original hand written signature.

APPRAISER

Signature_____
Name _____
Company Name _____
Company Address_____
_____
Telephone Number _____
Email Address_____
Date of Signature and Report _____
Effective Date of Appraisal _____
State Certification #_____
or State License #_____
or Other (describe) _____ State # _____
State _____
Expiration Date of Certification or License _____

ADDRESS OF PROPERTY APPRAISED
_____
_____
APPRAISED VALUE OF SUBJECT PROPERTY $ _____
LENDER/CLIENT
Name _____
Company Name _____
Company Address_____
_____
Email Address_____

SUPERVISORY APPRAISER (ONLY IF REQUIRED)

Signature_____
Name_____
Company Name _____
Company Address_____
_____
Telephone Number _____
Email Address_____
Date of Signature _____
State Certification #_____
or State License # _____
State _____
Expiration Date of Certification or License _____

SUBJECT PROPERTY

☐ Did not inspect subject property
☐ Did inspect exterior of subject property from street
    Date of Inspection _____
☐ Did inspect interior and exterior of subject property
    Date of Inspection _____

COMPARABLE SALES

☐ Did not inspect exterior of comparable sales from street
☐ Did inspect exterior of comparable sales from street
    Date of Inspection _____

Appendix
Calculating Area

A home appraisal generally requires the use of area in some way. Area is given in square units. When comparing properties, for example, you must be able to determine the size of a lot in square feet, the amount of floor space in a room or house, and the construction cost per square foot of various components of the house.

Many property boundaries and houses are irregularly shaped; that is, they are not rectangular. This appendix will show you how to compute the area of just about any shape that you might encounter.

AREA OF SQUARES AND RECTANGLES

The space inside a two-dimensional shape is its area. A right angle is the angle formed by one-fourth of a circle. Because a full circle is 360°, and one-fourth of 360° is 90°, a right angle is a 90° angle.

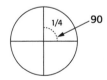

Squares and Rectangles

A rectangle is a closed figure with four sides that are at right angles to each other.

90°	90°
90°	90°

A square is a rectangle with four sides of equal length. A square with each side one inch long is a square inch. A square with each side one foot long is a square foot.

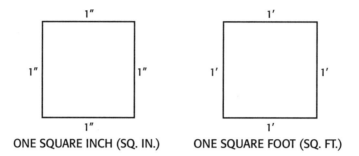

ONE SQUARE INCH (SQ. IN.)   ONE SQUARE FOOT (SQ. FT.)

Note: The symbol for *inch* is ". The symbol for *foot* is '. The abbreviations are *in.* and *ft.*

The area of a shape is the number of square units inside the shape. One way to find the number of square units in a shape is to place the shape on a larger number of square units and count the number of square units inside the shape.

The area of the square at the left, below, is four square inches.

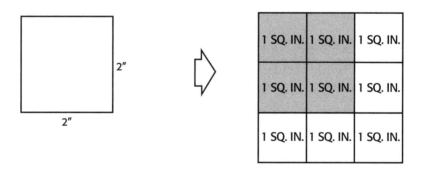

Counting squares is too cumbersome a method to use when dealing with large areas. The following formula may be used to compute the area of any rectangle:

$$\text{Area} = \text{Length} \times \text{Width, or}$$
$$A = L \times W$$

The area of the following rectangle, using the formula, is 5" × 6", or 30 square inches.

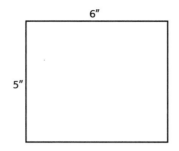

The term 30 inches refers to a straight line 30 inches long. The term *30 square inches* refers to the area of a specific figure. When inches are multiplied by inches, the answer will be in square inches. Likewise, when feet are multiplied by feet, the answer will be in square feet.

Square feet are sometimes expressed by using the exponent ^{2}; for example, 10^2 is read 10 feet squared and means $10' \times 10'$, or 100 square feet.

The exponent ^{2} indicates how many times the number, or unit of measurement, is multiplied by itself. This is called the *power* of the number or unit of measurement. The exponent is indicated at the upper right of the original number or unit of measurement.

The area of the rectangle at the left, below, is $4' \times 6'$, or 24 square feet. The area of the square at the right, below, is 5 yards $\times$ 5 yards, or 25 square yards.

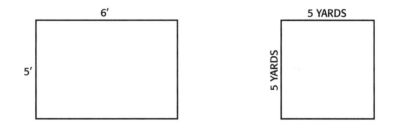

Example

Mr. Blair has leased a vacant lot that measures 60 by 160 feet. How much rent will he pay per year if the lot rents for $.75 per square foot per year?

Solution: To solve this problem, first compute the area of the lot:

$$A = L \times W = 160' \times 60' = 9,600 \text{ sq. ft.}$$

Then multiply the number of square feet by the price per square foot to calculate the total rent:

$$9{,}600 \times \$.75 = \$7{,}200$$

CONVERSIONS—USING LIKE MEASURES FOR AREA

When area is computed, all the dimensions used must be given in the *same kind of units.* When a formula is used to find area, units of the same kind must be used for each element of the formula, with the answer as square units of that kind. Thus, inches must be multiplied by inches to arrive at square inches, feet must be multiplied by feet to arrive at square feet, and yards must be multiplied by yards to arrive at square yards.

If the two dimensions to be multiplied are in different units of measure, one of the units of measure must be converted to the other. The following chart shows how to make these conversions:

12 inches = 1 foot

36 inches = 1 yard

3 feet = 1 yard

To convert *feet* to *inches,* multiply the number of feet by 12.	(ft. × 12 = in.)
To convert *inches* to *feet,* divide the number of inches by 12.	(in. ÷ 12 = ft.)
To convert *yards* to *feet,* multiply the number of yards by 3.	(yd. × 3 = ft.)
To convert *feet* to *yards,* divide the number of feet by 3.	(ft. ÷ 3 = yd.)
To convert *yards* to *inches,* multiply the number of yards by 36.	(yd. × 36 = in.)
To convert *inches* to *yards,* divide the number of inches by 36.	(in. ÷ 36 = yd.)

Example

Ms. Johnson's house is on a lot that is 75 feet by 1,500 inches. What is the area of the lot?

Solution: To solve this problem, first convert inches to feet:

$$1{,}500 \text{ inches} \div 12 = 125 \text{ feet}$$

Then compute the area of the lot:

$$A = L \times W = 75' \times 125' = 9{,}375 \text{ square feet}$$

To convert square inches, square feet, and square yards, use the following chart:

To convert *square feet* to *square inches*, multiply the number of square feet by 144.   (sq. ft. × 144 = sq. in.)

To convert *square inches* to *square feet*, divide the number of square inches by 144.   (sq. in. ÷ 144 = sq. ft.)

To convert *square yards* to *square feet*, multiply the number of square yards by 9.   (sq. yd. × 9 = sq. ft.)

To convert *square feet* to *square yards*, divide the number of square feet by 9.   (sq. ft. ÷ 9 = sq. yd.)

To convert *square yards* to *square inches*, multiply the number of square yards by 1,296.   (sq. yd. × 1,296 = sq. in.)

To convert *square inches* to *square yards*, divide the number of square inches by 1,296.   (sq. in. ÷ 1,296 = sq. yd.)

AREA OF TRIANGLES

A triangle is a closed figure with three straight sides and three angles. *Tri* means three.

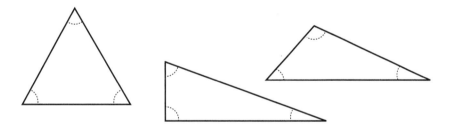

The two square-inch figure at the left, below, has been cut in half by a straight line drawn through its opposite corners to make two equal triangles. When one of the triangles is placed on a square-inch grid, it is seen to contain ½ sq. in. + ½ sq. in. + 1 sq. in., or 2 sq. in.

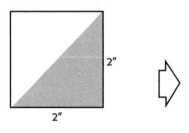

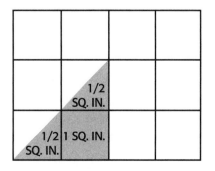

The area of the triangle below is 4.5 sq. ft.

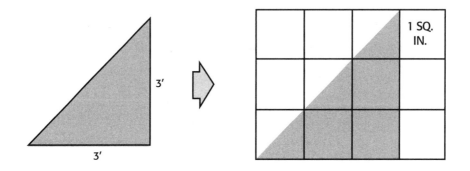

Again, the square-unit grid is too cumbersome for computing large areas. It is more convenient to use a formula for finding the area of a triangle:

Area of a Triangle = ½(Base × Height), or

A = ½(BH)

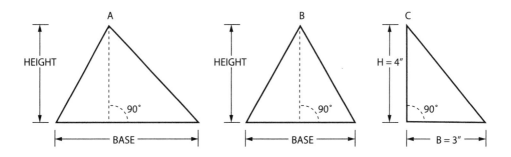

The base is the side on which the triangle sits. The height is the straight-line distance from the tip of the uppermost angle to the base. The height must form a 90° angle to the base. The area of triangle C above is as follows:

A = ½(BH) = ½(3″ × 4″) = ½(12 sq. in.) = 6 sq. in.

Example

The diagram on the next page shows a lakefront lot. Compute its area.

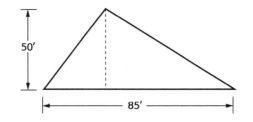

Solution: A = ½(BH) = ½(50′ × 85′) = ½(4,250 sq. ft.) = 2,125 sq. ft.

AREA OF IRREGULAR CLOSED FIGURES

Here is a drawing of two neighboring lots:

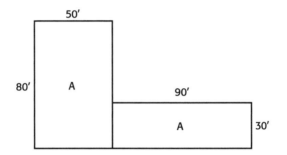

To find the total area of both lots:

$$\text{lot } A = 50' \times 80' = 4,000 \text{ sq. ft.}$$
$$\text{lot } B = 90' \times 30' = 2,700 \text{ sq. ft.}$$
$$\text{both lots} = 4,000 \text{ sq. ft.} + 2,700 \text{ sq. ft.} = 6,700 \text{ sq. ft.}$$

Two rectangles can be made by drawing one straight line inside figure 1, below. There are two possible positions for the added line, as shown in figures 2 and 3.

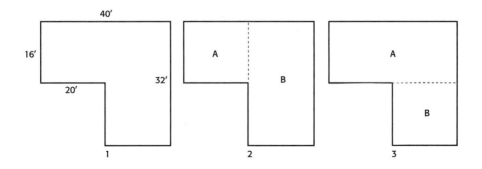

Using the measurements given in figure 1, the total area of the figure may be computed in one of two ways:

$$\text{Area of } A = 20' \times 16' = 320 \text{ sq. ft.}$$
$$\text{Area of } B = 32' \times (40' - 20') = 32' \times 20' = 640 \text{ sq. ft.}$$
$$\text{Total Area} = 320 \text{ sq. ft.} + 640 \text{ sq. ft.} = 960 \text{ sq. ft.}$$

Or:

$$\text{Area of } A = 40' \times 16' = 640 \text{ sq. ft.}$$
$$\text{Area of } B = (40' - 20') \times (32' - 16') = 20' \times 16' = 320 \text{ sq. ft.}$$
$$\text{Total Area} = 640 \text{ sq. ft.} + 320 \text{ sq. ft.} = 960 \text{ sq. ft.}$$

The area of an irregular figure can be found by dividing it into regular figures, computing the area of each regular figure, and adding all the areas together to obtain the total area.

Example

Compute the area of each section of the following figure. Then compute the total area.

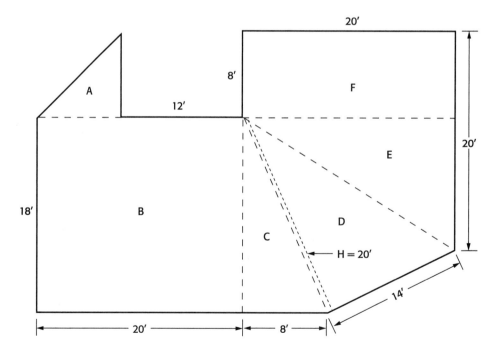

Solution: Area of A = ½ (20′ − 12′) × 8′ = 32 sq. ft.
        Area of B = 18′ × 20′ = 360 sq. ft.
        Area of C = ½(8′ × 18′) = 72 sq. ft.
        Area of D = ½(14′ × 20′) =140 sq. ft.
        Area of E = ½(20′ − 8′) × 20′ = 120 sq. ft.
        Area of F = 8′ × 20′ = 160 sq. ft.
        Total Area = 32 + 360 + 72 + 140 + 120 + 160 sq. ft. = 884 sq. ft.

LIVING AREA CALCULATIONS

Real estate appraisers frequently must compute the amount of living area in a house. The living area of a house is the area enclosed by the outside dimensions of the heated and air-conditioned portions of the house that are entirely above grade. This *excludes* open porches, garages, basements (even when finished and heated), unfinished attics, and the like.

When measuring a house to prepare for calculating the living area, these steps should be followed:

1. Draw a sketch of the foundation.
2. Measure *all* outside walls.
3. If the house has an attached garage, treat the inside garage walls that are common to the house as outside walls of the house.
4. Measure the garage.
5. Convert inches to twelfths of a foot (so that the same units of measurement are used in the calculations).
6. Before leaving the house, check to see that net dimensions of opposite sides are equal. If not, remeasure.
7. Section off your sketch into rectangles.
8. Calculate the area of each rectangle.
9. Add up the areas, being careful to *subtract* the area of the garage, if necessary.
10. Before leaving the house, *always* recheck the dimensions.

Example

What is the living area of the house shown in the sketch below? Follow steps 7–9 listed above.

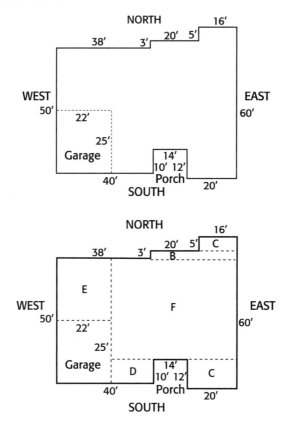

	Area		
Solution:	$A = 5' \times 16'$	=	80 sq. ft.
	$B = 3' \times (20' + 16') = 3' \times 36'$	=	108
	$C = 12' \times 20'$	=	240
	$D = 10' \times (40' - 22') = 10' \times 18'$	=	180
	$E = (50' - 25') \times 22' = 25' \times 22'$	=	550
	$F = (50' - 10') \times (74' - 22') = 40' \times 52'$	=	2,080
	TOTAL	=	3,238 sq. ft.

Glossary

AACI Accredited Appraiser Canadian Institute.

AAE Accredited Assessment Evaluator, International Association of Assessing Officers.

abatement The process by which an ad valorem real property tax assessment is stopped or reduced.

absolute fee simple title An unqualified right of ownership in real estate. Fee simple is the best title that can be possessed. Note that, even with fee simple title, there still may be some limitation on the use of the property. The limitation may be one that is publicly imposed, such as a zoning classification that allows only a stated property use, or the limitation may be privately imposed, such as a deed restriction that specifies architectural standards.

access The right to enter or leave a tract of land from a public way, which may be by an easement over land owned by someone else. Other terms that are used to refer to the right of access are *ingress* (right to enter) and *egress* (right to leave).

accessory buildings Structures that are secondary to the main building. On a residential lot, these might include a garage or storage shed.

accrued depreciation Total depreciation from the time of construction up to the time of appraisal.

accrued expenses Expenses incurred that are not yet payable.

acquisition appraisal An appraisal to determine the fair market value of property condemned for public use, to establish the compensation to be paid to the property owner.

acre A measure of land with a perimeter of approximately 209 feet by 209 feet; in area, 43,560 square feet or 160 square rods or 4,840 square yards.

actual age The total number of years elapsed since a structure was built. Also referred to as *historical* or *chronological age.*

adjustment Change to the sales price of a comparable property to account for a difference between the comparable and the property that is the subject of an appraisal. The sales price is increased by the value of any feature that is present in the subject but not in the comparable, but decreased by the value of any feature that is present in the comparable but not in the subject.

ad valorem Latin phrase meaning *according to value;* generally used to refer to any form of taxation based on the relative value of the things being taxed. Most real estate taxes are ad valorem taxes.

adverse land use A land use that has a detrimental effect on the market value of nearby properties.

aesthetic Relating to beauty, rather than to functional considerations.

AFA Association of Federal Appraisers.

age-life method Another name for the straight-line method of computing accrued depreciation.

AI Appraisal Institute.

AIC Appraisal Institute of Canada.

air rights The right to use the space above the physical surface of the land, generally allowing the surface to be used for some other purpose. Some air rights are transferable, allowing builders to combine air rights of several different properties to build a single high-rise structure.

allocation method Separation of the appraised total value of real estate between land and building. Allocation may be made by using a ratio or by subtracting a figure representing building value from the total appraised value of the property.

allowance for vacancy and collection losses The percentage of potential gross income that will be lost because of vacant units, collection losses, or both.

amenities In appraising, those property features that contribute to the owner's satisfaction and enjoyment of the property, particularly nonmonetary benefits, such as architectural excellence or scenic beauty.

anticipation, principle of The principle that the selling price of real estate is affected by the expectation of its future appeal and value.

appraisal An opinion of quantity, quality, or value and the process by which conclusions of property value are obtained. Also refers to the report setting forth the opinion of value and the process by which the opinion was reached.

appraisal methods The approaches used in the appraisal of real estate, including the cost approach, income capitalization approach, and sales comparison approach.

appraisal report An appraiser's written opinion to a client of the value of the subject property sought as of the date of the appraisal. A *form report* gives the most important details of the appraisal process in only a few pages, while a *narrative report* provides a comprehensive analysis of the data used to reach the opinion of value.

appraiser One who gives an opinion of value.

appreciation Increase in monetary value over time.

arm's-length transaction A transaction in which both the buyer and the seller act willingly and under no pressure, with knowledge of the present conditions and future potential of the property, and in which the property has been offered on the open market for a reasonable length of time with no unusual financing or other circumstances.

ASA American Society of Appraisers.

assessed value The value placed on land and buildings by a government entity (usually the assessor) for use in levying real estate taxes.

assessment The imposition of a tax, charge, or levy, usually according to established rates.

assessor The government official who determines property values for the purpose of ad valorem taxation, that is, taxation based on the relative value of property.

balance, principle of As applied to property uses, the principle that properties can reach their highest value when there are a sufficient number of complementary property types in the area; for instance, when the number of residential properties is adequate for the available retail facilities. A market is said to be in balance when there are somewhat more properties available for sale than there are buyers.

base rent The minimum rent payable under a percentage lease.

book value The value of a property as capital on the books of account; usually reproduction or replacement cost, plus additions to capital and less reserves for depreciation.

building capitalization rate The sum of the discount and capital recovery rates for a building.

building codes State laws or local ordinances specifying minimum building construction standards for the protection of public health and safety.

building residual technique A method of income capitalization using the net income remaining to the building after interest on land value has been deducted.

bundle of rights A term often applied to the rights of ownership of real estate, including the rights of using, renting, selling, or giving away the real estate or not taking any of these actions.

CAE Certified Assessment Evaluator, International Association of Assessing Officers.

capital Money or goods used to acquire other money or goods.

capitalization Determining the value of real estate by applying a desired rate of return to the property's expected annual net operating income, expressed as the following formula:

$$\frac{\text{Income}}{\text{Rate}} = \text{Value}$$

capitalization rate The rate that includes both a return on an investment as well as the return of the amount invested.

capitalized value method A method of computing depreciation by determining loss in rental value attributable to a depreciated item and applying a gross rent multiplier to that figure.

cash equivalency technique Method of adjusting a sales price downward to reflect the increase in value caused by the assumption or procurement by the buyer of a loan at an interest rate lower than the prevailing market rate.

change, principle of The principle that no physical or economic condition ever remains constant.

chattel Personal property items that are not considered part of the real estate on which they are located.

client One who hires another person as a representative or an agent for a fee.

compaction Matted down or compressed extra soil that may be added to a lot to fill in the low areas or raise the level of the parcel.

comparables Properties that are substantially equivalent to the subject property in their design, size, location, and quality of construction.

competition, principle of The principle that a successful business attracts other such businesses, which will dilute profits.

condemnation Taking private property for public use through court action under the government's right of eminent domain, with just compensation to the owner.

conditions, covenants, and restrictions (CC&Rs) Private limitations on property use placed in the deed received by the property owner, typically by reference to a Declaration of Restrictions recorded for an entire subdivision.

condominium The absolute ownership of space, referred to as a *unit,* generally in a multiunit building, by a legal description of the airspace that the unit actually occupies. Also included is an undivided interest in the ownership of the *common elements,* which are owned jointly with the other condominium unit owners. The condominium form of ownership is used both for residential and commercial properties.

conformity, principle of The principle that buildings should be similar in design, construction, and age to other buildings in the neighborhood to reach their highest value.

contiguous Adjacent parcels of land.

contract rent Rent being paid by agreement between lessor (landlord) and lessee (tenant).

contribution, principle of The principle that any improvement to property, whether to vacant land or to a building, is worth only what it adds to the property's market value, regardless of the improvement's construction cost.

cooperative A multiunit residential building with title in a trust or corporation that is owned by and operated for the benefit of persons living within it. These persons are the beneficial owners of the trust or the stockholders of the corporation, each possessing a proprietary lease.

cost approach The process of forming an opinion of the value of real estate by adding the appraiser's estimate of the reproduction or replacement cost of the property improvements, less the amount by which they have depreciated, to the land value.

cost index Number representing the construction cost at a particular time in relation to the cost at an earlier time, prepared by a cost-reporting or indexing service.

CPE Certified Personalty Evaluator, International Association of Assessing Officers.

cubic-foot method Method of estimating building reproduction cost by multiplying the number of cubic feet of space the building encloses by the current construction cost per cubic foot.

curable depreciation A depreciated item that can be restored or replaced economically.

data Information pertinent to a specific appraisal assignment. Data may be *general* (relating to the economy, region, city, and neighborhood) or *specific* (relating to the subject property and comparable properties in the market area).

decreasing returns, law of The principle that states that property reaches a point at which additional improvements no longer bring a corresponding increase in property income or value.

deed A written instrument that conveys title or an interest in real estate when executed and delivered properly.

deed restrictions Clauses in a deed to real estate limiting the future uses of the property. Deed restrictions may limit the number of buildings, their design, and the quality of their construction. Deed restrictions may affect the property rights appraised favorably or unfavorably, depending on existing uses of the subject and nearby properties.

depreciated cost The reproduction or replacement cost of a building, less accrued depreciation to the time of the appraisal.

depreciation Loss in value from any cause, including physical deterioration, functional obsolescence, and external obsolescence.

depth factor An adjustment factor applied to the value per front foot of lots that vary from the standard depth.

direct costs Construction costs that are involved with either site preparation or building construction, including fixtures.

disposal field A drainage area, which should not be close to the water supply, where waste from a septic tank is dispersed into the ground through tile and gravel.

easement A right to use the land of someone else for a specific purpose, such as a right-of-way or for utility lines. An easement is a *nonpossessory* interest in land; this means that the holder of an easement owns a right of use only and not any portion of the underlying land. An *easement appurtenant* passes with the land when the land is conveyed.

economic life The period of time during which a structure may reasonably be expected to perform the function for which it was designed or intended.

economic obsolescence (*See external obsolescence.*)

effective age The age of a building based on the actual wear and tear and maintenance, or lack of it, that the building has received.

effective gross income Income from all sources, less anticipated vacancy and collection losses.

egress The right to leave a tract of land to reach a public way.

eminent domain The right of a government or quasi-public body to acquire private property for public use through a court action called *condemnation*. The court determines whether the use is a public one and what the compensation paid to the owner should be.

encroachment A building, wall, or fence that extends beyond the land of the owner and illegally intrudes on the land of an adjoining owner or a public street or alley.

encumbrance Any lien (such as a mortgage, tax lien, or judgment lien), easement, restriction on the use of land, outstanding dower right, or other interest that may diminish the market value of real estate.

environmental obsolescence (*See external obsolescence.*)

equalization The raising or lowering of assessed values for real property tax purposes in a particular county or taxing district to make them equal to assessments in other counties or districts.

equity The interest or value that an owner has in real estate over and above any mortgage against it.

escalator clause A clause in a contract, lease, or mortgage providing for increases in wages, rent, or interest, based on fluctuations in certain economic indexes, costs, or taxes.

escheat The process by which the property of a decedent who dies *intestate* (without a will) and without heirs reverts to the state.

estate The degree, quantity, nature, and extent of interest that a person has in real estate.

excess income (*See* excess rent.)

excess rent The difference between the market rent and the contract rent, when the market rent is lower.

expense Outlay of money chargeable against income.

externalities, principle of The principle that holds that factors outside a property can influence property value. Outside factors that can affect property values range from upkeep of neighboring properties to economic and political factors, such as interest rates.

external obsolescence Loss in value from forces outside the building or property, such as changes in optimum land use, legislative enactments that restrict or impair property rights, and changes in supply-demand relationships. Also called *environmental* or *economic obsolescence.*

Federal Reserve bank system Central bank of the United States established to regulate the flow of money and the cost of credit (borrowing).

fee simple The greatest possible estate or right of ownership of real property, continuing without time limitation. Sometimes called *fee* or *fee simple absolute.*

FHA Federal Housing Administration; the institution that insures loans made by approved lenders in accordance with its regulations.

final opinion of value The appraiser's final opinion of the defined value of the subject property, arrived at by reconciling the values derived from the cost, income capitalization, and sales comparison approaches.

fixed expenses Those costs that are more or less permanent and do not vary in relation to the property's income, such as real estate taxes and insurance for fire, theft, and hazards.

fixture Anything attached to the land and considered part of the real estate, including things that once were personal property but are attached to real estate in such a way that they cannot be easily removed. An exception is made for *trade fixtures,* which are installed for commercial purposes under the terms of a lease and can be removed on termination of the lease.

foreclosure A court action initiated by the mortgagee (lender) or a lienor to have the court order that the debtor's real estate be sold to pay the mortgage or other lien, such as a mechanic's lien or judgment.

front foot A standard of measurement that is a strip of land one foot wide fronting on the street and extending the depth of the lot. Value may be quoted per front foot.

frost line The depth of frost penetration in the soil. The frost line varies through the United States, and foundation footings should be placed below this depth to prevent movement of the structure.

functional obsolescence Defects in a building or structure that detract from its value or marketability, usually the result of layout, design, or other features that are less desirable than features designed for the same functions in newer property. Functional obsolescence is described as *curable* when the physical or design features that are no longer considered desirable by property buyers can be replaced or redesigned at low cost. Functional obsolescence is described as *incurable* if the currently undesirable features are not easily remedied or economically justified.

gradient The slope, or rate of change in elevation, of a surface, road, or pipe. Gradient is expressed in inches of rise or fall per horizontal linear foot of ascent or descent.

gross income A property's total potential income from all sources during a specified period of time.

gross income multiplier (GIM) A figure used as a multiplier of the gross income of a property from all sources to produce an opinion of the property's value. Usually used with commercial real estate.

gross rent multiplier (GRM) A figure used as a multiplier of the gross rental income of a property to produce an opinion of the property's value. Usually used with single-family residences.

ground lease A lease for *land only* on which the tenant usually owns or is to construct a building, as specified by the lease. Such leases are usually long-term net leases; that is, the tenant pays all or most of the expenses associated with ownership of the real estate, such as property taxes.

GSA Graduate Senior Appraiser, National Residential Appraisers Institute.

highest and best use Historically, the legally and physically possible use of land that produces the highest land (or property) value. A *highest and best use study* considers the balance of site and improvements as well as the intensity and length of nearby uses.

historical cost Actual cost of a building at the time it was constructed.

historical rent Contract rent paid in past years.

HUD Department of Housing and Urban Development.

IAAO International Association of Assessing Officers.

IFA Member, National Association of Independent Fee Appraisers, Inc.

improvements on land Alterations or structures of whatever nature, usually privately rather than publicly owned, erected on a site to enable its utilization; for example, buildings, fences, driveways, and retaining walls.

improvement to land Usually a public work, or one publicly dedicated, such as a curb, sidewalk, street lighting system, or sewer, constructed to enable the development of privately owned land.

income capitalization approach The process of estimating the value of an income-producing property by capitalization of the annual net operating income expected to be produced by the property during its remaining useful life.

increasing returns, law of The principle that additional property improvements increase property income or value.

incurable depreciation A depreciated item that would be impossible or too expensive to restore or replace.

indirect costs Construction costs that do not involve either site preparation or building erection; for example, the building permit, land survey, overhead expenses such as insurance and payroll taxes, and builder's profit.

industrial district or park A controlled, parklike development designed to accommodate specific types of industry, providing public utilities, streets, railroad sidings, water, and sewage facilities.

ingress The right to enter a tract of land. Often used interchangeably with the term *access.*

installment contract A contract for the sale of real estate by which the purchase price is paid in installments over an extended period of time by the purchaser, who is in possession, with the title retained by the seller until a certain number of payments are made.

interest The cost of credit. A percentage of the principal amount of a loan charged by a lender for its use, usually expressed as an annual rate.

interest rate Return of an investment, consisting of four component rates: *safe rate* (interest rate paid on investments of maximum security, highest liquidity, and minimum risk); *risk rate* (addition to safe rate to compensate for the hazards that accompany investments in real estate); *nonliquidity rate* (penalty charged for the time needed to convert real estate into cash); and *management rate* (compensation to the owner for the work involved in managing an investment and reinvesting the funds received from the property).

land The earth's surface in its natural condition, extending down to the center of the globe, including all things affixed to it and the airspace above the surface to navigable airspace.

land capitalization rate The rate of return, including interest on the land only.

landlocked parcel A parcel of land without access to any type of public road.

landlord One who owns property and leases it to a tenant. Also called the *lessor.*

land residual method A method of capitalization using the net income remaining to the land after return on and recapture of the building value have been deducted.

latent defect Physical deficiency or construction defect not readily ascertainable from a reasonable inspection of the property, such as a defective septic tank or underground sewage system, or improper plumbing or electrical wiring.

lease A written or oral contract for the possession of a landlord's (lessor's) property for a stipulated period of time in consideration for the payment of rent by the tenant (lessee). Leases for more than one year generally must be in writing,

legal description A statement identifying land by a system prescribed by law.

levy To impose or assess a tax on a person or property; the amount of taxes to be imposed in a given district.

loft An atticlike space below the roof of a house or barn; any of the upper stories of a warehouse or factory.

lot and block system A method of legal description of an individual parcel of land by reference to tract, block, and lot numbers and other information by which the parcel is identified on a recorded subdivision map. Also called *lot, block, and tract system* or *subdivision system.*

MAI Member designation of the Appraisal Institute.

maintenance expenses Costs incurred for day-to-day upkeep, such as management wages and benefits of building employees, fuel, utility services, decorating, and repairs.

market price (*See sales price.*)

market rent An estimate of a property's rent potential, that is, what an investor can expect to receive in rental income.

market value The most probable price real estate should bring in a sale occurring under normal market conditions.

mechanic's lien A lien created by statute that exists in favor of contractors, laborers, or materialmen who have performed work or furnished materials in the erection or repair of a building. It also includes architects, engineers, landscapers, and truckers.

metes and bounds system A method of legal description specifying the perimeter of a parcel of land by use of measured distances from a point of beginning along specified boundaries, or bounds, using monuments or markers as points of reference.

MFLA Master Farm and Land Appraiser, National Association of Master Appraisers.

mile A measurement of distance; equivalent to 1,760 yards or 5,280 feet.

mobile home A structure transportable in one or more sections, designed and equipped to contain not more than two dwelling units to be used with or without a foundation system; does not include a recreational vehicle. Also called a *manufactured home.*

NAIFA National Association of Independent Fee Appraisers, Inc.

NAR National Association of REALTORS®.

neighborhood A residential or commercial area with similar types of properties, buildings of similar value or age, predominant land-use activities, and natural or fabricated geographic boundaries, such as highways or rivers.

neighborhood life cycle The period during which most of the properties in a neighborhood undergo the following three stages: *development* (growth), in which improvements are made and properties experience rising demand and value; *equilibrium,* in which properties undergo little change; and *decline,* in which properties become less desirable and require an increasing amount of upkeep to retain their original utility.

net lease A lease requiring the tenant to pay rent and all the costs of maintaining the building, including property taxes, insurance, repairs, and other expenses of ownership. Sometimes known as an *absolute net lease* or *triple net lease.*

net operating income Income remaining after operating expenses are deducted from effective gross income.

nonconforming use A property use that is permitted to continue after a zoning ordinance prohibiting it has been established for the area; a use that differs sharply from the prevailing uses in a neighborhood.

observed-condition method A method of computing depreciation in which the appraiser estimates the loss in value for all items of depreciation.

obsolescence Lessening of value from out-of-date features (property design, construction materials, or use) that are no longer desired by property buyers. Obsolescence is an element of depreciation.

occupancy rate The percentage of total rental units occupied and producing income.

operating expenses The cost of all goods and services used or consumed in the process of obtaining and maintaining income. (*See* maintenance expenses, fixed expenses, and reserves for replacement.)

operating statement The written record of a business's gross income, expenses, and resulting net income.

option A right given for a valuable consideration to purchase or lease property at a future date for a specified price and terms. The right may or may not be exercised at the option holder's discretion.

orientation Positioning a structure on its lot considering its exposure to the sun and prevailing winds and the need for privacy and protection from noise.

overall capitalization rate The direct ratio between a property's annual net income and its sales price.

overimprovement An improvement to property that is not likely to contribute its cost to the total market value of the property.

percentage lease A lease commonly used for commercial property that provides for a rental based on the tenant's gross sales on the premises. It generally stipulates a base monthly rental, plus a percentage of any gross sales exceeding a certain amount.

personal property Movable objects called *chattel* that are not permanently attached to real estate and thus are not transferred when the real estate is sold.

physical deterioration—curable Loss of value caused by neglected repair or maintenance that is economically feasible to cure and would result in an increase in market value equal to or exceeding the cost to cure.

physical deterioration—incurable Loss of value caused by neglected repairs or maintenance of building components that would not contribute comparable value to a building if corrected.

physical life The length of time a structure can physically exist without regard to its economic use.

planned unit development (PUD) A subdivision consisting of individually owned residential and/or commercial parcels or lots as well as areas owned in common.

plottage value The subsequent increase in the unit values of a group of adjacent properties when they are combined into one property. Also called *assemblage.*

point of beginning The place at which a legal description of land starts, using the metes and bounds method.

prepaid items of expense Expense items, such as insurance premiums and tax reserves, that have been paid in advance of the time that the expense is incurred. Prepaid expenses are prorated and credited to the seller when preparing a closing statement.

price The amount of money set or paid as the consideration in the sale of an item at a particular time.

profit and loss statement (*See* operating statement.)

progression, principle of The principle that states that the value of a property will be greater when it is surrounded by properties that are in better condition than it would be if it is surrounded by properties in equally good or worse condition.

property residual technique A method of capitalization using the net operating income remaining to the property as a whole.

quantity survey method A method for finding the reproduction cost of a building in which the costs of erecting or installing all of the component parts of a new building, including both direct and indirect costs, are added.

real estate Land; a portion of the earth's surface extending downward to the center of the earth and upward into space, including fixtures permanently attached thereto by nature or by man, anything incidental or appurtenant to land, and anything immovable by law.

real property The rights of ownership associated with real estate. Also used interchangeably with the term *real estate.*

recapture rate The percentage of a property's original cost that is returned to the owner as income during the remaining economic life of the investment.

reconciliation The final step in the appraisal process in which the appraiser reconciles the estimates of value received from the cost, income capitalization, and sales comparison approaches to value to arrive at a final estimate of market value for the subject property.

reconstruction of the operating statement The process of eliminating the inapplicable types of expense items for appraisal purposes and adjusting the remaining valid expenses, if necessary.

rectangular survey system A method of legal description of real estate, established in 1785 by the federal government, by which land is referenced by proximity to *principal meridians* and *baselines*. Also called the *U.S. government survey system* and the *section and township system*.

regional multipliers Adjustment factors by which standard cost figures can be multiplied to allow for regional price differences.

regression, principle of The principle that states that the value of property will not be as great when it is surrounded by properties that are in poorer condition as it would be if it is surrounded by properties in equally good or better condition.

remaining economic life The number of years of useful life left to a building from the date of appraisal; that is, the remaining number of years in which it can be used for its intended purpose.

rent-loss method of depreciation *(See* capitalized value method.)

replacement cost The current construction cost of a building with exactly the same utility as the subject property.

reproduction cost The current construction cost of an exact duplicate of the subject building, using the same materials and techniques.

reserves for replacement Allowances set up for replacement of building and equipment items that have a relatively short life expectancy.

residual In appraising, the value remaining after all deductions have been made.

right-of-way The right that one has to pass across the land of another; an *easement*.

risk rate *(See* interest rate.)

rod A measure of length; 16½ feet.

safe rate (*See* interest rate.)

sales comparison approach The process of forming an opinion of the market value of property through the examination and comparison of actual sales of comparable properties. Also called the *market data approach.*

sales price The actual selling price of a property.

site Land suitable for building purposes, usually through the addition of utilities or other services.

special assessment A charge against real estate made by a unit of government to cover the proportionate cost of an improvement, such as a street or sewer.

special purpose property Property that has unique usage requirements, such as a church or a museum, making it difficult to convert to another use.

square foot method A method for finding the reproduction cost of a building in which the cost per square foot of a recently built comparable structure is multiplied by the number of square feet in the subject property.

SRA Senior Residential Appraiser designation, Appraisal Institute.

SR/WA Senior Right of Way Agent designation, International Right of Way Association.

straight-line method A method of computing depreciation in which the cost of a building is depreciated at a fixed annual percentage rate. Also called the *age-life method.*

straight-line recapture A method of capital recapture in which total accrued depreciation is spread over the useful life of a building in equal amounts.

subdivision A tract of land divided by the owner into blocks, building lots, and streets by a recorded subdivision plat. Compliance with local regulations is required.

substitution, principle of The basic appraisal premise that the market value of real estate is influenced by the cost of acquiring a substitute or comparable property.

summation method Another term for the cost approach to appraising.

supply and demand, principle of The principle that the value of a commodity will rise as demand increases and/or supply decreases.

survey The process of measuring land to determine its size, location, and physical description. Also, the map or plat showing the results of a survey.

tenant One who has possession of real estate. In the broad sense, an owner of any kind of right or title (tenant in common); in the limited sense, a lessee (month-to-month tenant). The estate or interest held is called a *tenancy*.

time-share An estate (ownership) or use interest in real property for only a designated time period each year, usually measured in weekly increments. Because of high initial marketing costs, time-share units in some areas have shown little or no appreciation at the time of resale.

title The evidence of a person's right to the ownership and possession of land.

topography Surface features of land; includes elevation, ridges, slope, and contour.

trade fixtures Articles of personal property installed by a tenant under the terms of a lease. Trade fixtures are removable by the tenant before the lease expires.

underimprovement An improvement to real estate that is less than the property's highest and best use; for example, a single-family house built on a lot zoned for a six-unit residential building.

unit-in-place method A method for finding the reproduction cost of a building in which the construction cost per square foot of each component part of the subject building (including material, labor, overhead, and builder's profit) is multiplied by the number of square feet of the component part in the subject building.

useful life The period of time during which a structure may reasonably be expected to perform the function for which it was designed or intended.

use value The value of a property designed to fit the specific requirements of the owner but that would have little or no use to another owner. Also referred to as *value-in-use*.

vacancy and collection losses (*See* allowance for vacancy and collection losses.)

valuation principles Factors that affect market value, such as the principles of substitution, highest and best use, supply and demand, conformity, progression, regression, contribution, increasing and decreasing returns, competition, change, stage of life cycle, and anticipation.

value The power to command other goods in exchange; the present worth of future rights to income and benefits arising from ownership.

vendee Buyer.

vendor Seller.

way A street, alley, or other thoroughfare or easement permanently established for passage of persons or vehicles.

yield Income on an investment. Usually used to refer to equity investments.

zoning ordinance Regulation of the character and use of property by a municipality or county through the exercise of its police power.

Index